Cheryl Malkowski

doodle quilting MANIA

250+ new Free-Motion Designs

for Blocks, Borders, Sashing & More

Publisher: Amy Marson

Creative Director: Gailen Runge

Acquisitions Editor: Roxane Cerda

Managing Editor: Liz Aneloski

Editor: Kathryn Patterson

Technical Editor: Linda Johnson

Cover/Book Designer: April Mostek

Production Coordinator: Tim Manibusan

Production Editor: Alice Mace Nakanishi

Illustrators: Cheryl Malkowski and Mary E. Flynn

Photo Assistant: Rachel Holmes

Photography by Kelly Burgoyne of C&T Publishing, Inc., unless otherwise noted

Published by C&T Publishing, Inc., P.O. Box 1456, Lafayette, CA 94549

Library of Congress Cataloging-in-Publication Data

Names: Malkowski, Cheryl, 1955-, author.

Title: Doodle quilting mania : 250+ new free-motion designs for blocks, borders, sashing & more / Cheryl Malkowski.

Description: Lafayette, CA : C&T Publishing, Inc., [2019]

Identifiers: LCCN 2018046690 | ISBN 9781617457951 (softcover : alk. paper)

Subjects: LCSH: Machine quilting--Patterns.

Classification: LCC TT835 .M271747 2019 | DDC 746.46--dc23

LC record available at https://lccn.loc.gov/2018046690

Printed in China

10 9 8 7 6 5 4 3 2 1

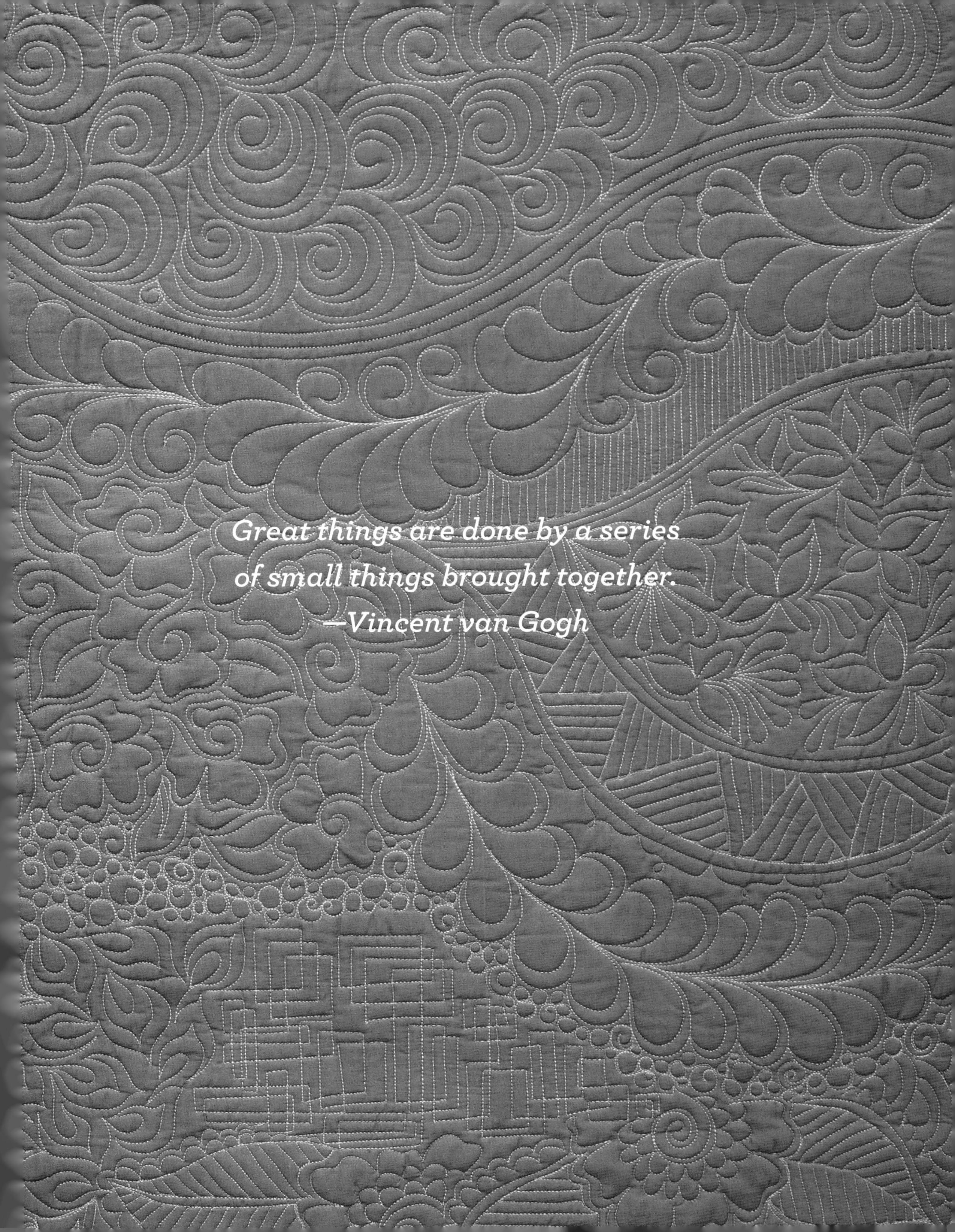

Great things are done by a series of small things brought together.

—Vincent van Gogh

Contents

Introduction

This book builds on the foundation of understanding and drawing quilting motifs that was presented in my previous book, *Doodle Quilting* (page 127). The concept is simple: Every design can be broken down into basic shapes that anyone can learn to draw—with a bit of practice! We can all write our names, so that is our starting point—the simple shapes that form cursive letters. We also need to understand how motifs work together and how individual shapes behave while drawing them out. Knowing these things will enable us to solve the problem of where to go next in our quilting, which I believe is the biggest struggle most quilters face.

Doodle Quilting Mania expands on that foundation by adding more of everything! There are more Travelers (page 8), which are the shapes that will get you from one place to another. These shapes are incorporated into every other motif presented, so learning how to draw them every which way is vitally important. There are more Boomerangs (page 16), which are motifs in which the starting and ending points are the same—a shape that generally does not lend itself to being repeated on its own to fill a space. Included in these are flowers, leaves, feathers, and other motifs found in nature and architecture. There are more Ensembles (page 30), where Boomerangs and Travelers are strung together to make an interesting pattern to fill an area or a whole quilt.

To make things even more interesting, included in this book are some design ideas for specific traditional blocks, sashing, borders, and even layouts for Radiant Lone Star and Chain settings with more or less plain alternating blocks.

I recommend using Premium Clear Vinyl (by C&T Publishing) and a dry-erase pen to trace over motifs that may be causing you grief, just to get the muscle memory going in your hand. If you are having trouble with anything presented here, it's a great idea to go back to tracing, and practice, practice, practice!

Since we are now going beyond the basics, some designs will require a bit of prep work. Each motif is clearly noted when it is necessary to pre-mark or use a ruler. For example, you can pre-mark gentle curves that you want to keep consistent with chalk or with an air- or water-soluble pen, or use a straight or curved ruler. Learning to use a ruler on a longarm or domestic machine is a valuable skill that will serve you well. There are some great books written on the topic, including *Rulerwork Quilting Idea Book* by Amanda Murphy (from C&T Publishing), so I won't go into it here. I have also found sets of rolls of painter's tape in widths from ¼″ to ¾″ that are useful for guiding straight lines. Sometimes it is necessary to just mark where a motif will be centered, so you can get them spread evenly over an area. This is all the marking I ever do, so it's all the help I can be!

You will notice that there are a lot of designs that can be used in places besides where they are suggested in this book, especially the block designs. My hope is that you will freely mix, match, and otherwise shake up what I'm presenting. Most importantly, I hope you have fun, because that's why we do this in the first place, right?

More Travelers

trav•el•er (noun) [tra´-və-lər, trav´-lər]—
one who journeys to a specific place

These motifs enable you to move around your quilt, meaning they can be repeated to make an allover pattern or be a building block in a closed design. Truly, they are the foundational tools for quilters!

note

The Legend (page 125) gives an overview of the basic designs first presented in *Doodle Quilting* (page 127). Refer to it often to refresh your memory or to see what I'm referring to.

Single Direction S-Curves

A variation of the letter S, the key to making these work is being sure that when you switch direction for the next S, you are touching the previous S. Sometimes you will need to make a long, exaggerated point to close the gap.

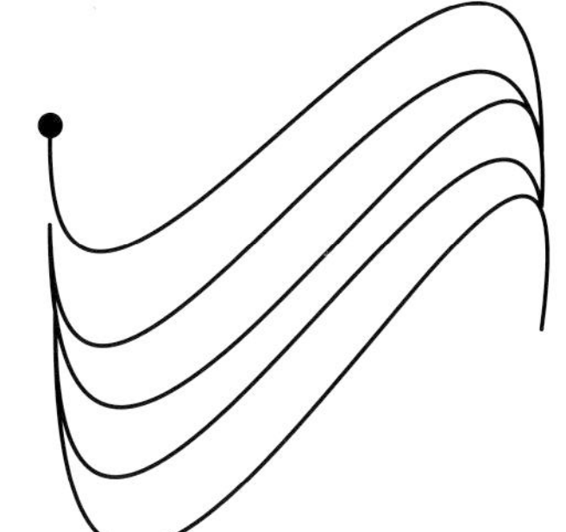

Rain-in-a-Puddle

Think of this as the Bark motif that rotates around an imaginary center. The key is to work around that center, being sure to leave yourself room to get out to finish the outside and get onto the next motif. Try tracing around this a few times to get the idea.

Tornados

Tornados are made just like Rain-in-a-Puddle, only using points when you change direction.

Random Direction S-Curves

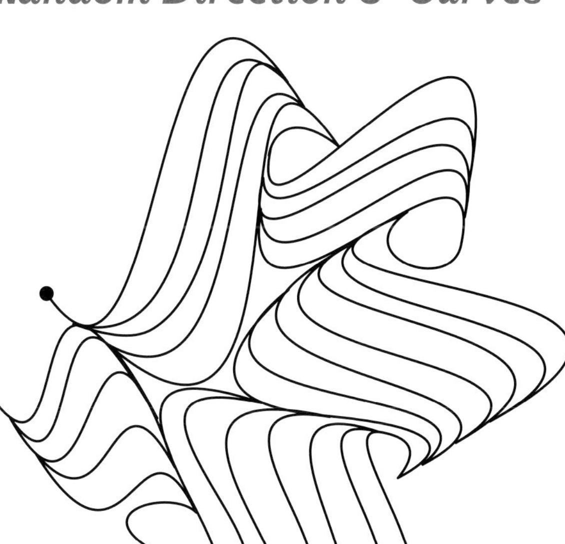

Once you have a little row of S-Curves, curl around at the end of the last S and start off again in a new direction, remembering to keep the ends closed and butting up against a previous line whenever possible.

Triple Vine

Make a slightly curvy line, then double back, exaggerating the curves and crossing the lines, then do it once more before continuing on.

Orange Peel

A very shallow C-curve that usually is used to go from point to point in a pieced design. Always keep your eyes on the next point when quilting this to help land precisely at the point!

Note: I refer to the line in blue as a Diagonal Orange Peel.

Bouncing Curves

These are Orange Peels cut loose in a less formal setting, bouncing back and forth and changing direction. As with the S-Curve, keep the ends closed or butted against an adjacent line.

Curved Spikeys

Even more liberated are the Curved Spikeys, which are the same curves, except they don't bother to button up at the points.

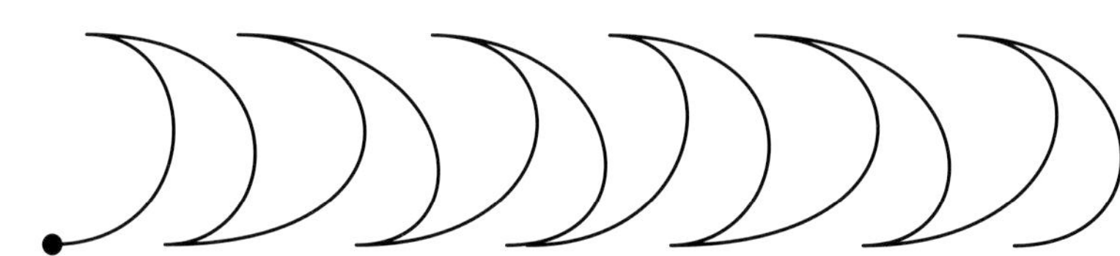

Rainbows

Start with a small arc, then travel along the base to where you would like to make a larger arc that echoes the first. Make as many echoes as you want. Then start again using the previous rainbow(s) as a boundary.

Traveling Ovals

Ovals can travel, just like circles!

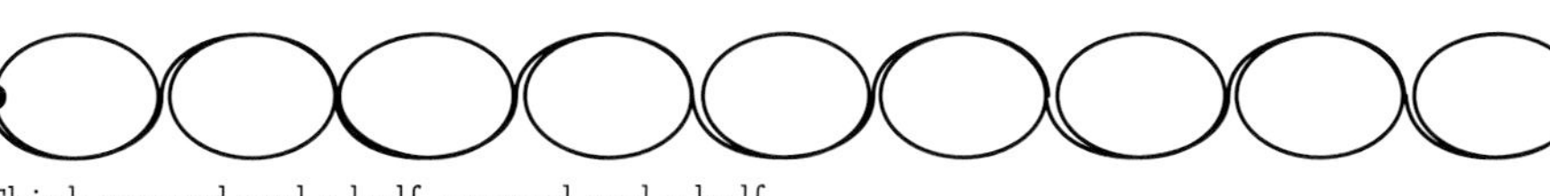

Think around and a half, around and a half.

Traveling Diamonds

A Traveling Diamond is really just 4 Orange Peel arcs where the ends of the arcs touch to form a diamond. To make them travel, backtrack over 2 arcs to reach the next diamond.

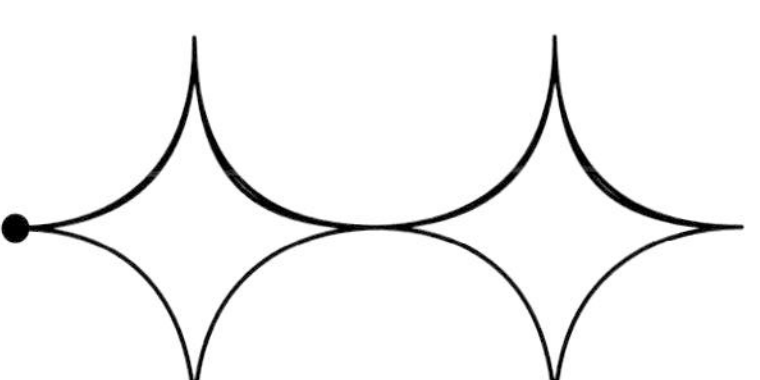

Overlapping Circles

Do you need permission to scribble like you are four years old again? You can control these and make them equally overlapped, or be silly and mix them up!

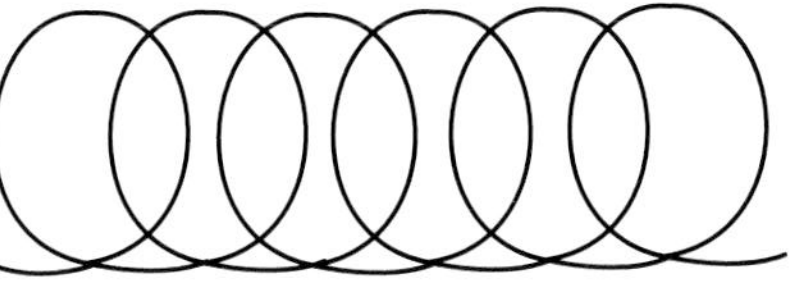

Pointed Double Hook

This is a variation on a Double Hook, which is often used as a feather substitute with the bonus of *no backtracking*!

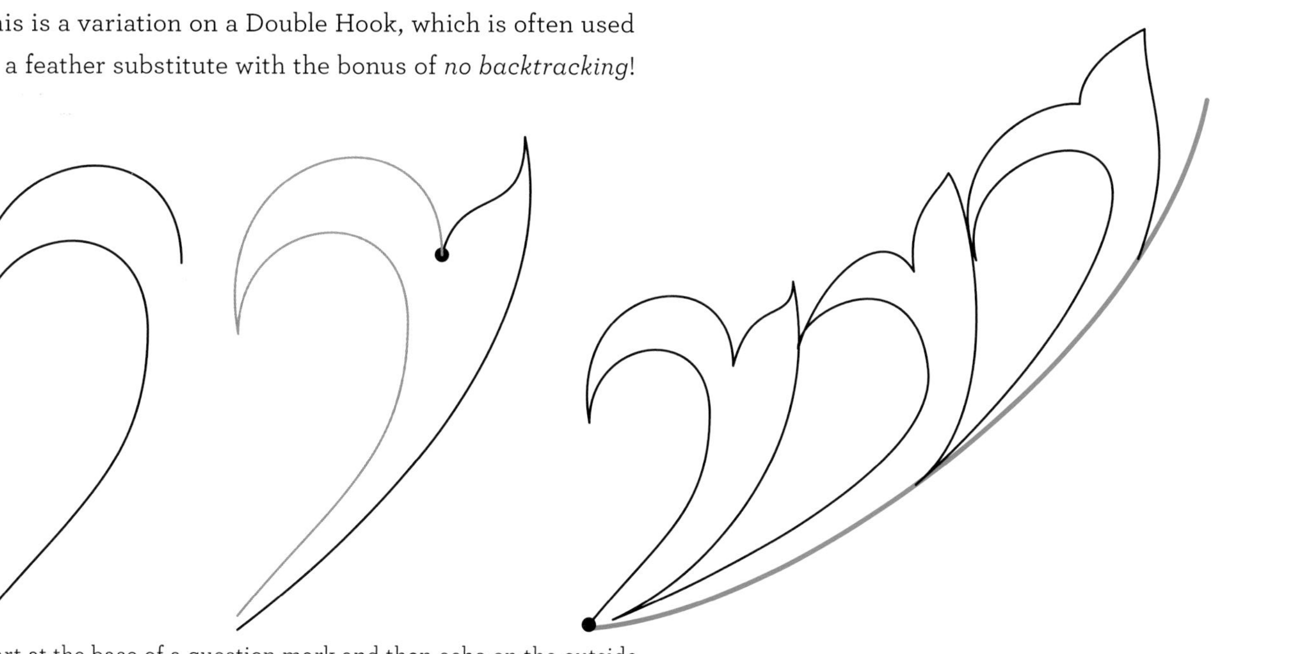

Start at the base of a question mark and then echo on the outside, almost even with the first upward stroke. Then change direction and make a little Sunshine point before returning to the base. Think up and around, back, point, and down.

The Comma

Another feather substitute, think of it like you were tracing around the outside of a printed comma.

Think up, stop, around, and down.

Square Loop Vine

This is like a loop vine, only with no curves and random-sized rectangles.

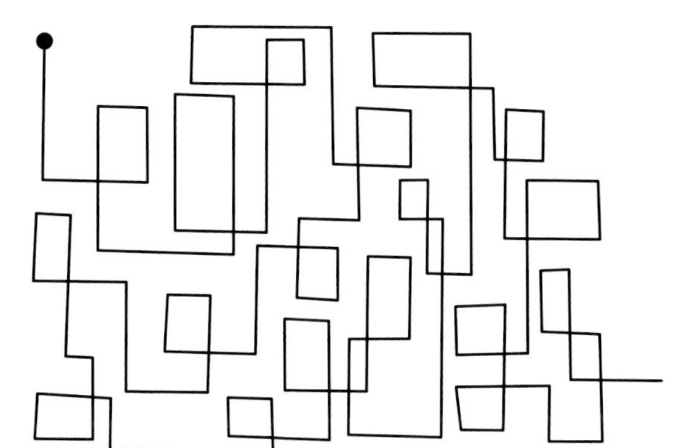

Overlapping Squares

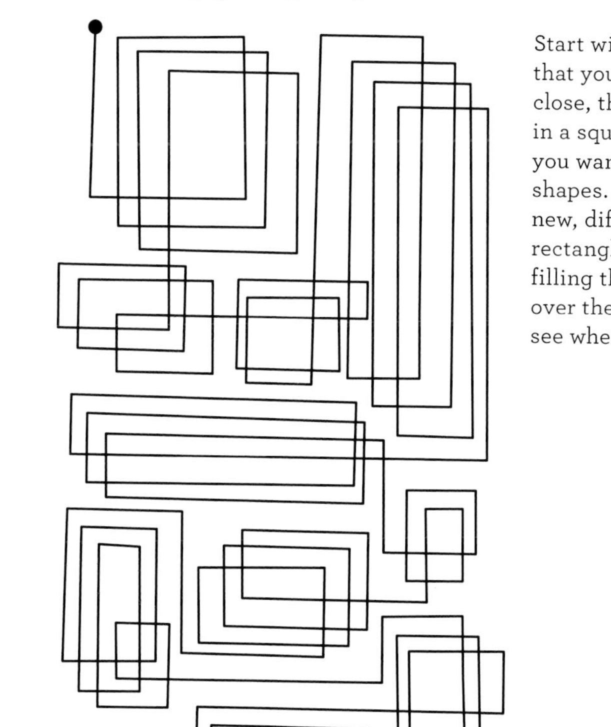

Start with a rectangle that you don't quite close, then continue in a square spiral until you want to change shapes. Then start a new, different-sized rectangle and repeat, filling the area. Trace over the example to see where it goes.

Random Greek Keys

Change up Greek Keys so there are a lot of different shapes and sizes!

Herringbone

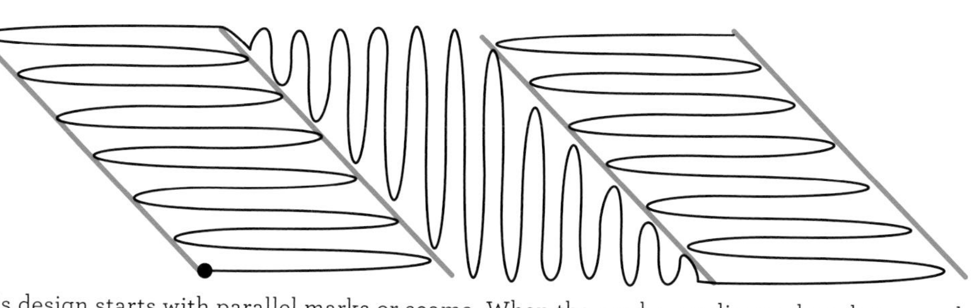

This design starts with parallel marks or seams. When the marks are diagonal as shown, make a straight horizontal line inside the boundaries, then a tight curve, and reverse directions. Continue to the end of the space and in the next set of boundaries, make the lines vertical.

Jagged Meander

Think of this as meandering with no curves.

Teardrop 1–2–3 Variation—Sunshines

Remember the Teardrop 1–2–3 motif from *Doodle Quilting*? Try varying it by making the second and third passes a pointed Sunshine.

Teardrop 1–2–3 Variation—Leaves

Try using a small, simple no vein leaf as the basis for the 1–2–3 motif.

Budded Scrolls

This is a variation of the C's or Scrolls introduced in *Doodle Quilting*. The difference is that, instead of always doubling back on the outside of the C, most of the time, go to the inside and add little tufts of leaves or Curved Spikeys, and once in a while, add one to the outside of the C as well. This motif deserves some practice time!

More Boomerangs

boo•mer•ang (noun) [bü´-mər-aŋ]—

a device that, when used properly, returns to the point of origin

Here are some shapes to help keep your quilting interesting. Use the concepts laid out in *Doodle Quilting* and all the Travelers (page 8) to master these motifs!

Flowers

So many flowers and variations in the quilting world!

BLEEDING HEART

Think out and around like a heart, flip like a 60's hairstyle, back to the middle, down to a point, then mirror image on the way back up.

ROSE BUD

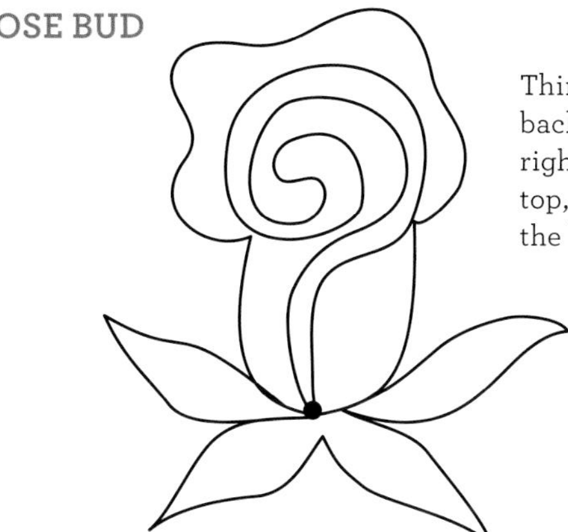

Think question mark, echo back to base, up to kiss the right side, curves around the top, kiss the left side, down to the base, then 4 simple leaves.

SPIRAL FLOWER

Think in to the center, Swirly, Curved Spikey petals around the center, with a thin vein running almost to the end of each petal.

CLEMATIS

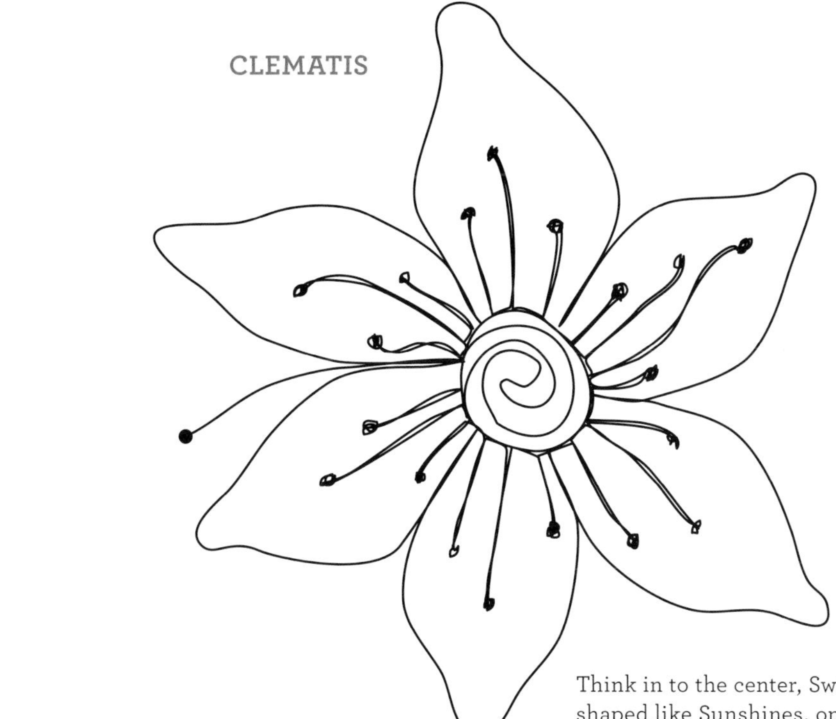

Think in to the center, Swirly, then petals shaped like Sunshines, only round on top, keep the walls of the petals together part way up, then make 3 or 4 curvy stamens with scribbles on the ends in each petal.

DOUBLE HOOK FLOWER

Think big question mark out, echo back in, small question mark out, echo back in.

DOUBLE HOOK FLOWER WITH CENTER

Think into the center, round, then fat question marks that echo back to center. Then travel along the center circle to start the next petal.

DOUBLE HOOK FLOWER 2

Think fat question mark out, echo back in, and so on, getting the point where you reverse as close to the previous line as possible.

DOUBLE TEARDROP FLOWER

Make teardrops with echoes that rotate around the center of the flower.

PEONY BUD

Start with a fairly large circle. On the inside, make 3 or 4 inward-facing Teeth from *Doodle Quilting* with sides touching. Travel to the outside of the circle and make 5 or 6 Teeth petals, maybe having some with points in the middle.

PEACOCK FLOWER

From the center of the flower, make an upright 1-2-3 Teardrop Variation, then 2 more smaller, partial motifs that lie flat at the base. Add a long, skinny Comma to each side going up and Double Hooks facing down.

LILY

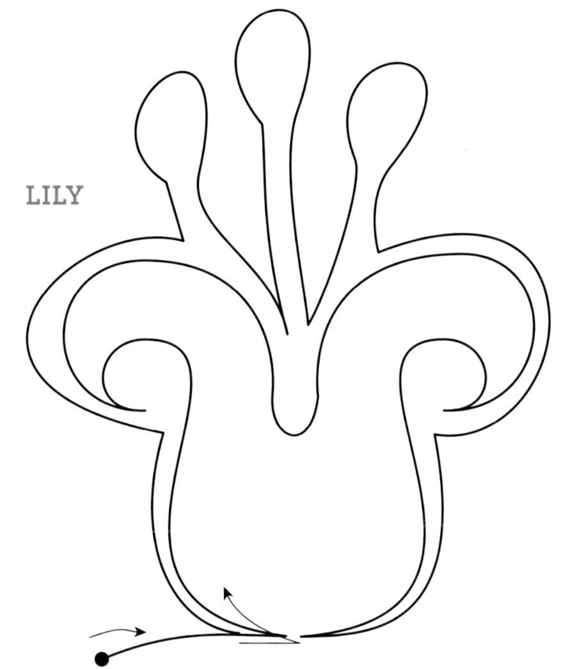

Think about making an upside down 60's flip hairstyle or fat conjoined Double Hooks to start. From the base, go up with a curvy question mark, stop, echo back about halfway down before making a tight curve and a mirror image to the base. Then closely echo up to the top where you add the stamens, which is like tracing around 3 lollipops. Echo back to the base.

PEA POD

Think gentle curve and up to a point, come back, cross over, and add continuous loops along the first curve.

SEED POD

Think smashed oval, the 3 Sunshine petals, then echo.

SWIRLY SEED POD

Think round center, Swirly, then 3 or 4 Sunshine petals.

WINTER BERRIES

Think of these as a bunch of teardrops that refuse to close at the top and keep pulling away. Group together as many as you'd like.

CORNFLOWER

Go into the middle, make long, thin Sunshine petals that rotate around the center, then the larger outside petals with spiky ends.

FUCHSIA BUD

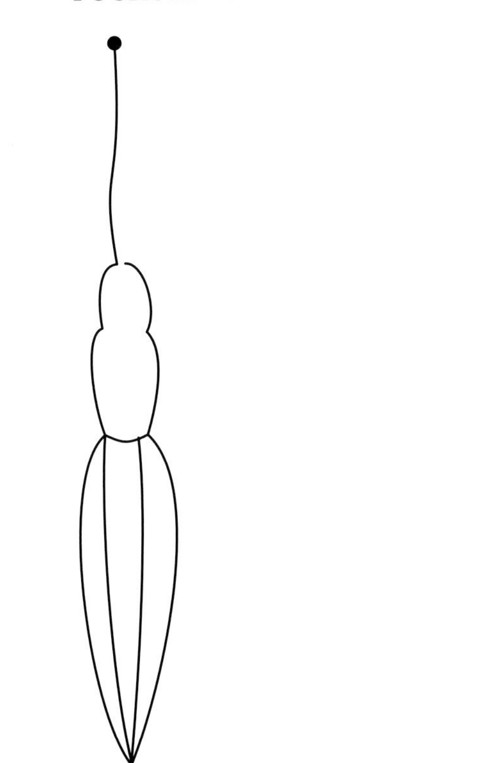

Think, starting at the top, small bump, longer bump, much longer bump, point, reflect the longest bump on the other side. Go just a bit toward the middle of the bud, then make a deep V that goes all the way down to the tip. Stitch back to the top of that long bump, then go up to reflect the 2 top bumps. Phew!

FUCHSIA

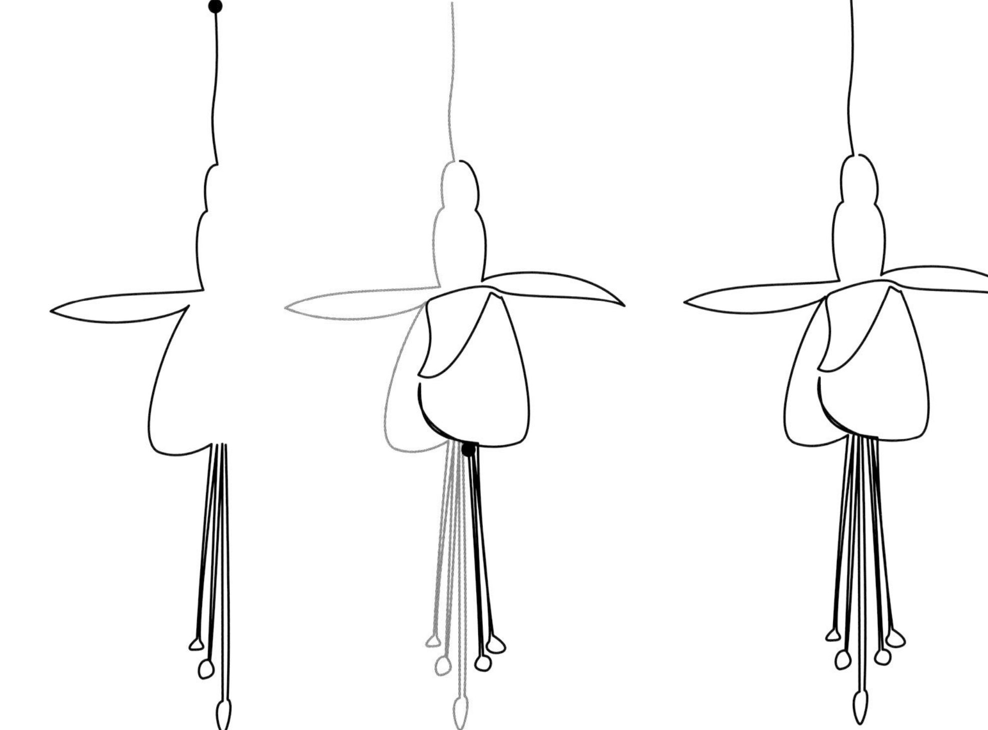

Start just like the Fuchsia Bud with the 2 bumps, then go out with a little wing, back almost to where you start, then make a bottom-heavy C and add downward stamens. Make a gentle curve upward and to the left, and backtrack to establish the petals. More stamens, then swing up to the left, backtrack, and mirror the C-curve back up. Angle over a tiny bit, then make a downward-facing, almost triangle-shaped petal that eases back up into the wing on the right and finally the 2 bumps.

CHRYSANTHEMUM

Go into the center, make an oval and echo inside it. Inside that, follow the oval contours to make a ring of Traveling Circles. Travel back outside the ovals and make a full ring of Flower Petals, then narrowly echo all the way back. Backtrack on that last echo, as shown by #1. At #2, change direction and make 3 petals on the right side. At #3, start on the next ring of petal that go almost to the top. Echo back to that same #3 petal, reversing directions with the last row of petals and echoing to finish out up on the top right of the flower.

TUFTED ZINNIA

Go into the center, make a circle with a Swirly, then 2 rows of small flower petals, travel out to make larger Tooth Petals all around and finish with a narrow echo.

DANDELION PUFF PLANT

From the base, go to the center of the puff and make radiating lines of varying lengths with an asterisk on the end of each one. Then go back down the stem and make 2 opposing leaves, like really long Oak leaves.

DANDELION FLOWER

There are a lot of petals in this, but they are just long, skinny Tooth petals that radiate around the center.

DANDELION SEED

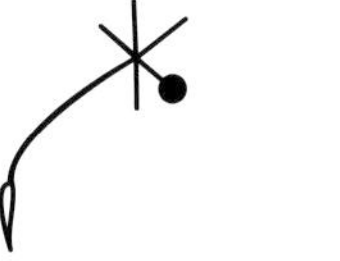

Think asterisk, vine, tiny teardrop.

YOUNG DANDELION

Start from the top of the stem. Think down and back, oval, simple leaves around the bottom and 2 rows of long skinny Tooth petals coming out from the top.

Leaves

Here are more leaves to add to your palette!

BUMPY LEAF

Think in and back and flower petals all around.

CHRYSANTHEMUM LEAF

Start by drawing veins that are swollen, like you are tracing around cotton swabs, then echo those veins around the leaf, making a point at the top.

HALF BUMPY LEAF

Think in and back and 2 more veins, then make a fan with 3 bumps on top.

SWIRLY LEAF

Start at the base and make this leaf like a tall Sunshine. Halfway down the second side, stop, and make a Swirly before continuing on.

HEART LEAF

Like a heart that goes down too far in the middle.

PINE TREE

Make the trunk of the tree out of a rectangle with only 3 sides. Then swing out to make Curved Spikeys on the right that lean to the right. As you come to the other side of the tree, make the Spikeys curve to the left. Go back and forth, making each row narrower as you get to the top.

S-CURVE LEAF

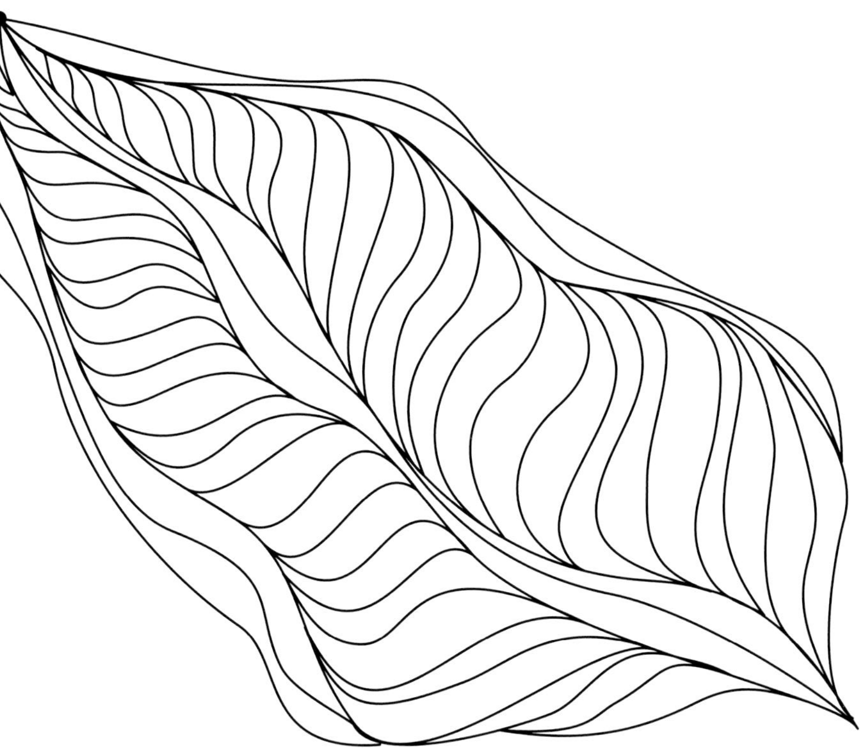

Start at the top and go to the base of the leaf with 3 wavy lines that meet at the beginning and end. Then start making S-Curves up one side, making sure the points are closed, getting narrower as you go toward the top. Repeat down the opposite side, getting wider as you go to the bottom. Backtrack along the outside edges of the S-Curves on both sides of the leaves, then echo twice with randomly wavy lines.

JUNGLE LEAF

Start by marking where you want your vein. Then, begin at the base and draw a nice fat football-leaf shape. Once you're back at the base, travel up the vein a short distance and echo the bottom of the leaf to the outside edge. Backtrack along the outside a short distance and echo again back to the vein. Continue all the way up and when you're coming back down, echo first on the outside of the leaf so when you come to the vein, you complete that section of the vein. Continue echoing all the way to the base.

FRILLY JUNGLE LEAF

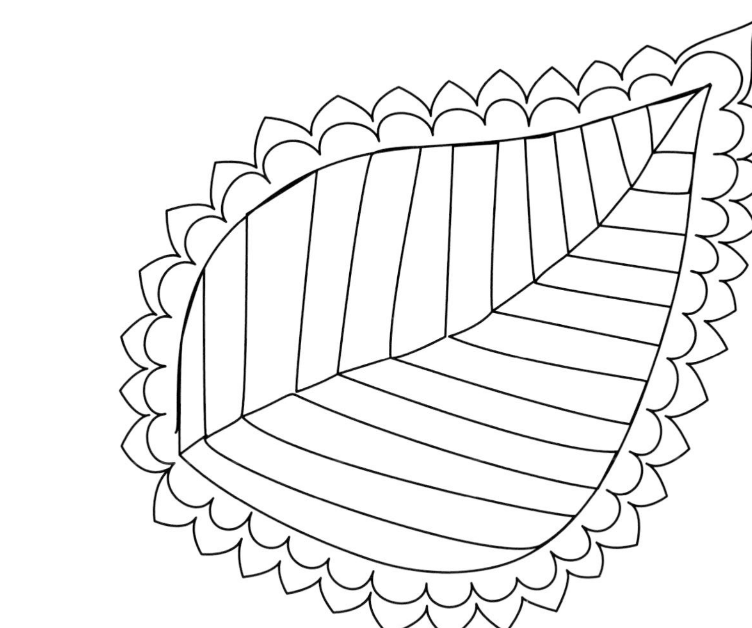

To the Jungle Leaf above, add a row of small Flower Petals and a row of Sunshines.

Bugs and Miscellaneous Boomerangs

DRAGONFLY

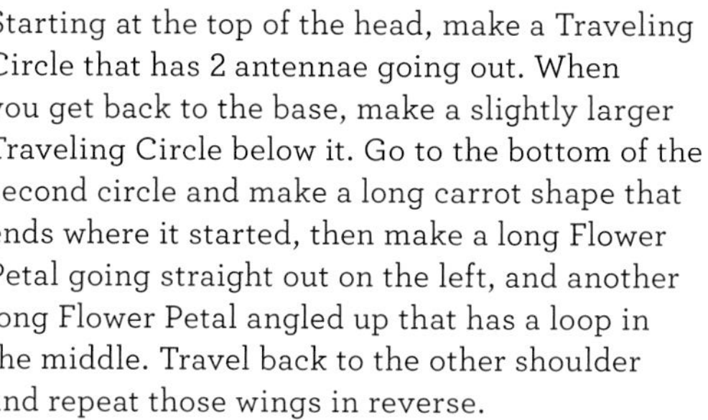

Starting at the top of the head, make a Traveling Circle that has 2 antennae going out. When you get back to the base, make a slightly larger Traveling Circle below it. Go to the bottom of the second circle and make a long carrot shape that ends where it started, then make a long Flower Petal going straight out on the left, and another long Flower Petal angled up that has a loop in the middle. Travel back to the other shoulder and repeat those wings in reverse.

BUTTERFLY

Come up from the bottom with a long, barely arched curve, then add a head and come back down. Make a point and backtrack a little way up one side of the body. The lower and upper wings are like really badly drawn hearts, so make one small and one larger so that you end up near the shoulder. Backtrack around the head and add antennae, then make mirror images of the wings.

SIDE VIEW BUTTERFLY

Make a long, skinny Comma, pausing at the top for 2 antennae. When you get back to the starting point, backtrack about a third of the way up the back of the body and make wings like for a regular butterfly starting at the bottom of the wing. When you reach the top, pretend you are drawing the same shape, but a lot of it is hidden, so angle it up a bit and when you kiss the front wing, backtrack until another bit bumps out, backtrack, and make one more bump.

BOOMERANG DIAMONDS

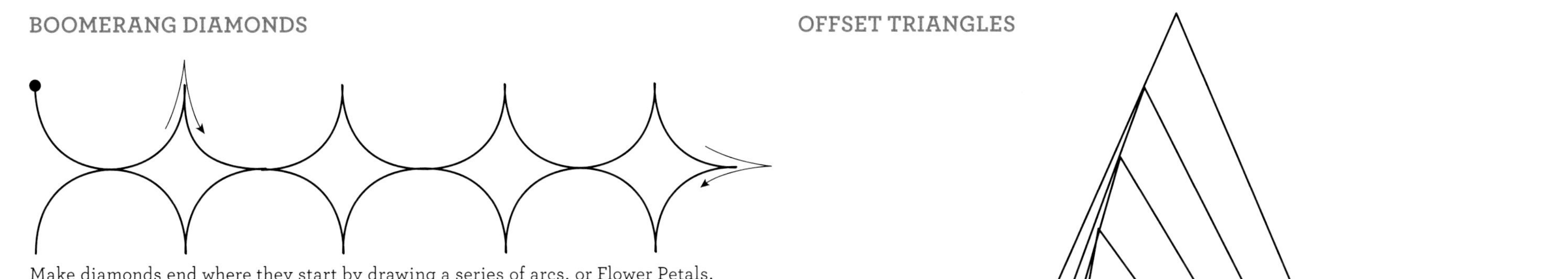

Make diamonds end where they start by drawing a series of arcs, or Flower Petals, ending with half an arc, then reversing and going back to the beginning, drawing the arcs upside down so that the tops of the arcs touch and the points are lined up.

CLOUDS

Start with a flat bottom to your cloud, then make some continuous Flower Petals. Echo back to the bottom of the cloud and start making bigger Flower Petals until you get to the bottom again. Add a quick Curved Spikey and return to the beginning. You can change these up and get some really fun cloud shapes!

OFFSET TRIANGLES

Starting in the middle of the space, draw a triangle, but go a bit past the point where the triangle closes. Stop, then make a straight line that kisses the next corner and goes a bit past. Continue in the same manner until the space is filled.

More Ensembles

en•sem•ble (noun) [än-säm´-bəl]—
a unit or group of complementary parts that contribute to a single effect

A successful Ensemble, or allover design, combines a group of Travelers, Boomerangs, or both that enhance the quilt top. These can be employed to cover a whole quilt or a particular space on a quilt. These are my favorite quilt patterns for everyday quilts because they are easy to use, without starts and stops, and still add interest to the quilt.

Designs

HOOKS + PETALS + ECHOING

DOUBLE HOOKS + PETALS + ECHOING

DOUBLE HOOKS + TOOTH PETALS + SIMPLE LEAVES + ECHOING

BUDDED SCROLLS + LEAVES

SWIRLY SEED PODS + ECHOING

This one is squared off so you can have an example of how to fit a design into a space.

SEED PODS + WINTER BERRIES + ECHOING

DOUBLE HOOKS + ECHOING

TRAVELING CIRCLES + ROUND SWIRLIES

RIBBONS + SIMPLE LEAVES

Add the leaves in when the lines cross on your return trip.

TEARDROP 1-2-3'S + SPIKEYS

TRIPLE VINES + SEED PODS + ECHOING

Start with a triple vine and connect each Seed Pod at the side or bottom.

DOUBLE HOOKS + CURVED SPIKEYS

CHRISTMAS TREES + LOOPED VINES + STARS

VINES + TEARDROPS

This works best when you go out to the end of a vine and add the teardrops as you backtrack along that vine.

PEACOCK FLOWERS + LOOPED VINES + DOUBLE HOOKS + PEAS

TRIPLE VINES + LEAVES + DOUBLE HOOK FLOWERS

LINES + LEAVES

LINES + TRAVELING CIRCLES

LINES + HEARTS

Make these hearts travel by restitching one side.

LINES + DAISIES

Backtrack around flower center to continue.

SWIRLIES + VICTORIAN FEATHERS

You can use nearly any of the Travelers to replace the on-the-line backtracking between feather fronds in a Victorian Feather. Then use that Traveler to fill empty spaces. Here are two examples.

Swirlies + Victorian Feathers + Traveling Circles

Use Traveling Circles instead of backtracking to travel from one feather to the next.

Swirlies + Victorian Feathers + Curved Spikeys

Use Spikeys instead of backtracking to travel from one feather to the next.

SCROLLS + RAINBOWS

ELEGANT SCROLLS

This is similar to Budded Scrolls (page 15), but it is looser; the lines that make the sides of the vine never touch, but they sometimes overlap.

DOUBLE HOOKS + FEATHERS

Make 3 Double Hooks in a row, bring the end of the final Hook back to the base of the feather, and continue with feathers up the opposite side.

SKY: DOUBLE HOOKS + RAINBOWS + CLOUDS + ECHOING

EXCITED WATER + LILIES + RAINBOWS + SWIRLIES + HEART LEAVES + SPIKEYS + ECHOING

CHRYSANTHEMUM FLOWERS AND LEAVES + S-CURVES

Dividing Your Space

Using a line to divide up your quilting space results in some interesting designs. Here are a few ideas, free-form and diagonal.

TRAVELING CIRCLES + STRAIGHT VINES

DIVIDED SPIKEYS

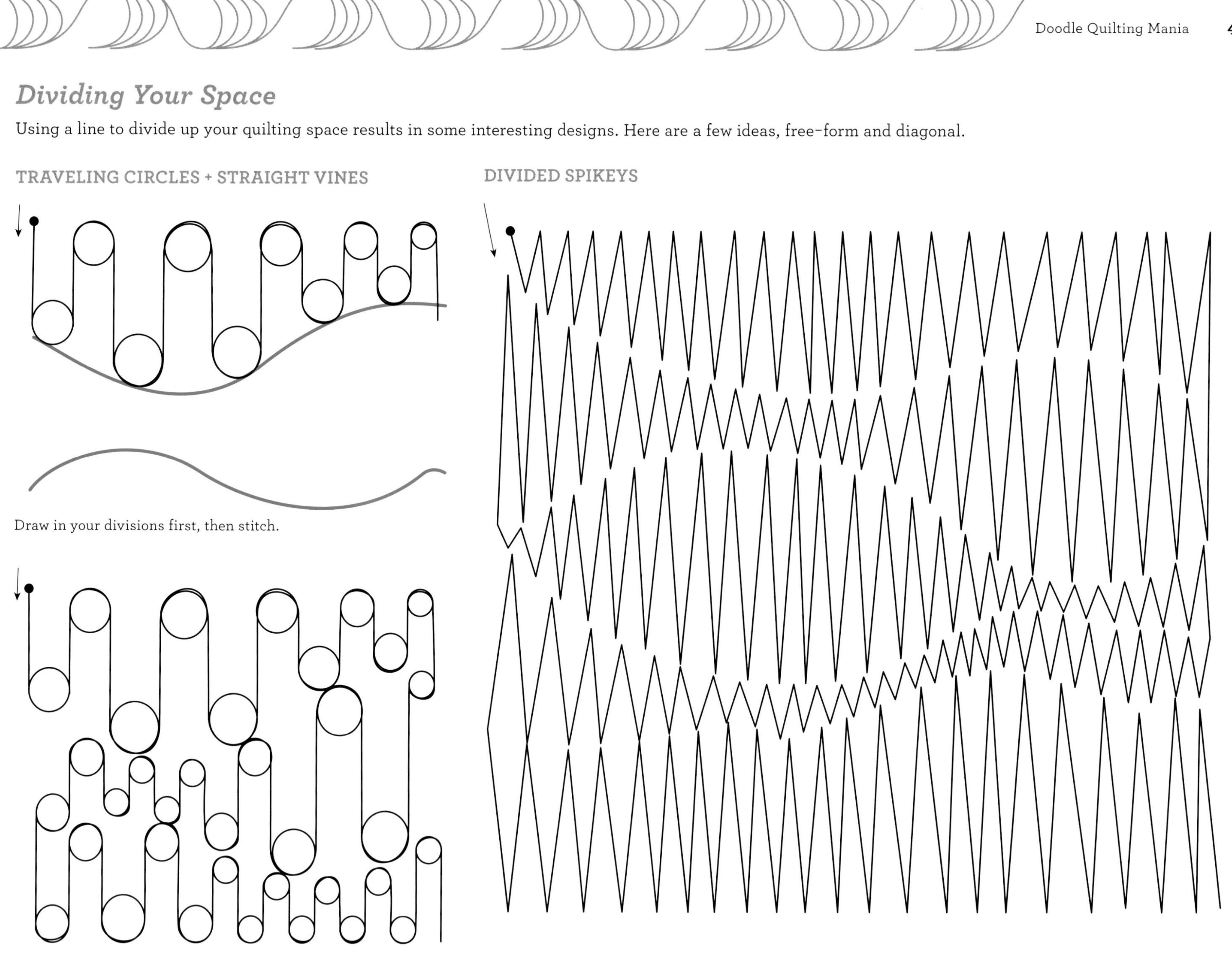

Draw in your divisions first, then stitch.

SCROLLS + LINES + SWIRLIES + FINGER FEATHERS

Stitch straight lines between each diagonal element. This would be a good design with which to use the varying sizes of freezer tape for marking lines.

WAVY LINES + ECHOING

You can use your piecing seam-lines as a guide to keep the spacing consistent.

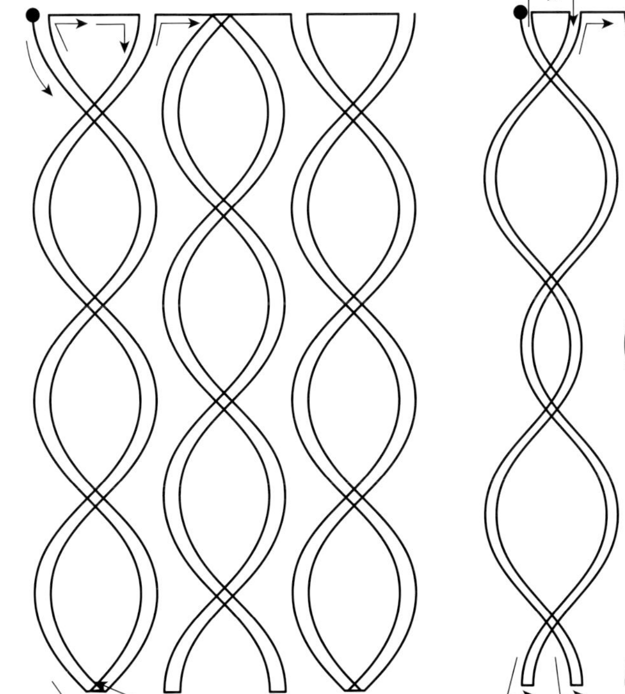

OFFSET WAVY LINES + ECHOING

Vary the distance between the wavy line sets to change up the design.

WAVY LINES + ECHOING + SWIRLIES + SIMPLE LEAVES

Set up your wavy lines so that the sides touch, echo, then, as you close a shape, add the leaves and Swirly, backtrack down the stem and continue the Wavy Line.

WAVY LINES + ECHOING + PALM FERNIES

As you close the shapes in a column, go up through the middle of the shapes making one half of the Palm Ferny, then go back down and complete the other side. Continue on with the Wavy Lines.

TRIPLE VINES + FUCHSIAS + LEAVES + VINES

Approach this design by making the shapes with the Triple Vines first, then adding in columns of fuchsias or leaves connected by vines. Almost any Boomerang could be used here.

TRIPLE VINES + DOUBLE TEARDROP FLOWERS + VINES

Adding Motifs to Change a Design

DOUBLE HOOKS + ECHOING

Start with a basic design like this one, and add in Traveling Circles or Feathers or something else altogether to make really interesting quilting designs.

DOUBLE HOOKS + ECHOING + TRAVELING CIRCLES

DOUBLE HOOKS + ECHOING + VICTORIAN FEATHERS

Ideas for Quilting Individual Blocks

This chapter is divided according to the type of block, such as a Nine-Patch or a Four-Patch, or the grid. You will find that some of the designs are interchangeable, as they repeat in every square. Try them out on different blocks with the same grid!

The designs are meant to fill one block, so you may need to start and stop between blocks, or even within a block. Sometimes you will find a need to travel around the outside of the block along the seamline in order to complete the motif. So, while they are not as quick as an allover design, they can give your quilt a more custom look.

Four-Patch Designs

ORANGE PEELS + STITCH-IN-THE-DITCH

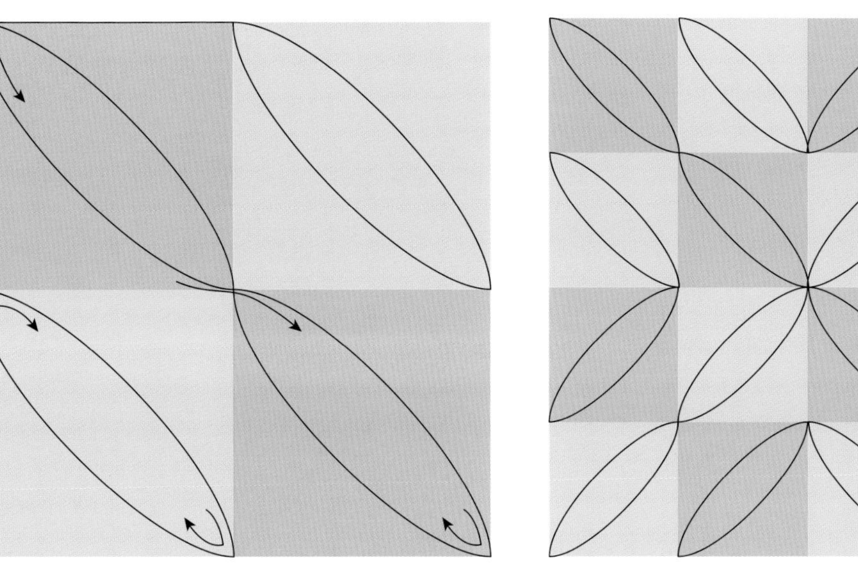

Use diagonal points in each square as the start and turn points. If necessary, travel along seam to the next square.

HOOKS + S-CURVES

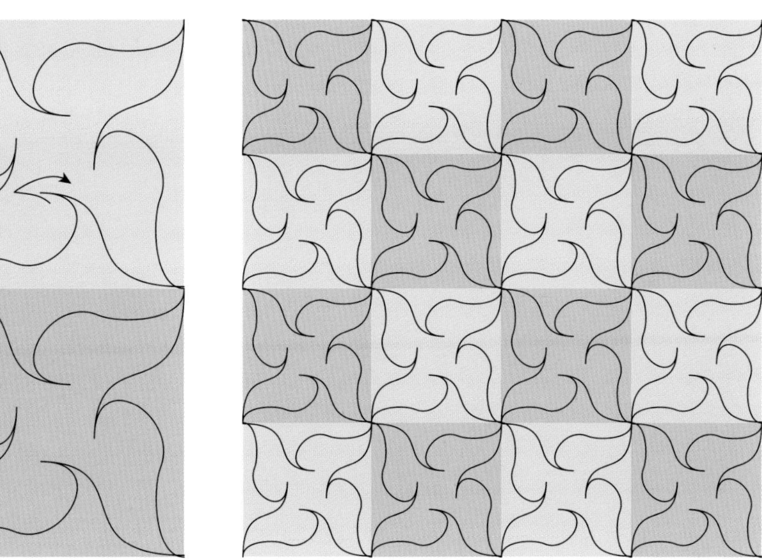

OPPOSING S-CURVES

Technically called a Brace.

DIAGONAL ORANGE PEELS + REFLECTING CONTINUOUS CURVES

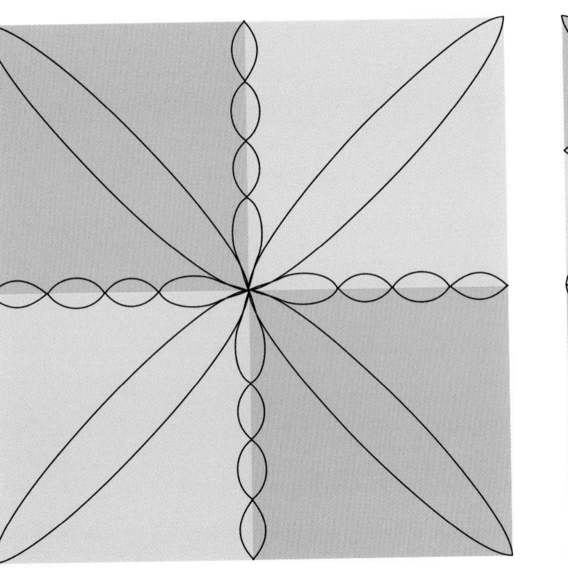

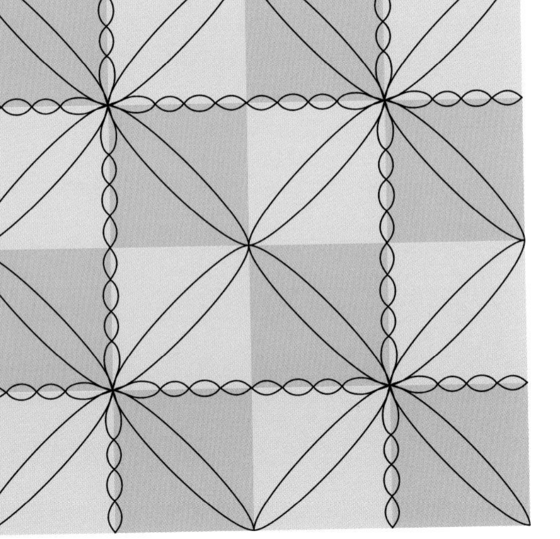

Start at any corner and make all the Orange Peels and then all the little footballs by making a consistent curve and reflecting it when doubling back.

ORANGE PEELS + STRAIGHT LINES

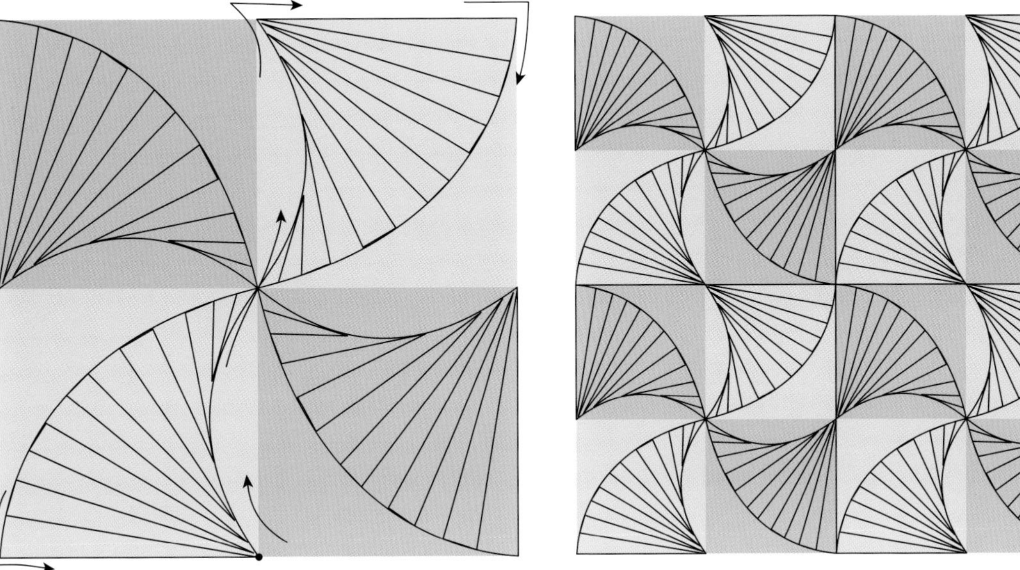

Start with 2 Orange Peels along the center of the Four-Patch, stitch straight to the outside edge of the block, then make half of a Diagonal Orange Peel (page 10) back to the bottom of the block, and return to the starting point. Then begin making straight lines at regular intervals between the 2 lines you've made. Repeat in the squares on the other diagonal.

TEARDROPS + ECHOING

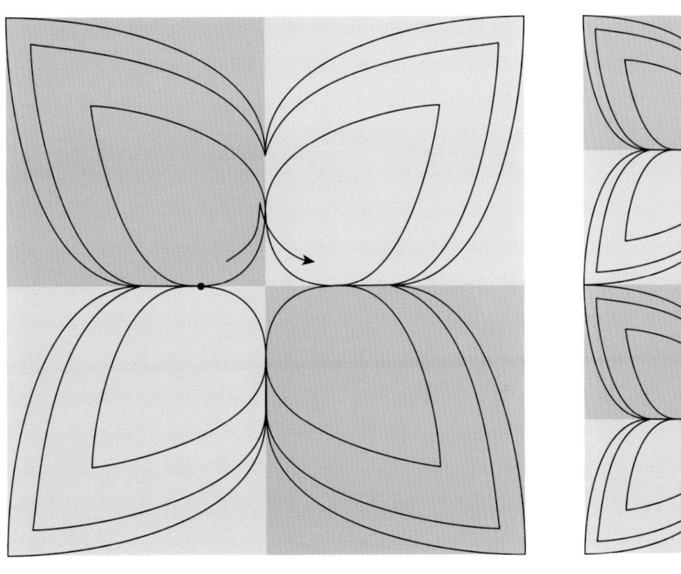

Start slightly away from the center along a seam. Make a curve-sided diamond. Complete each Teardrop around the center, travel away along the seam and echo twice.

SUNSHINE PETALS

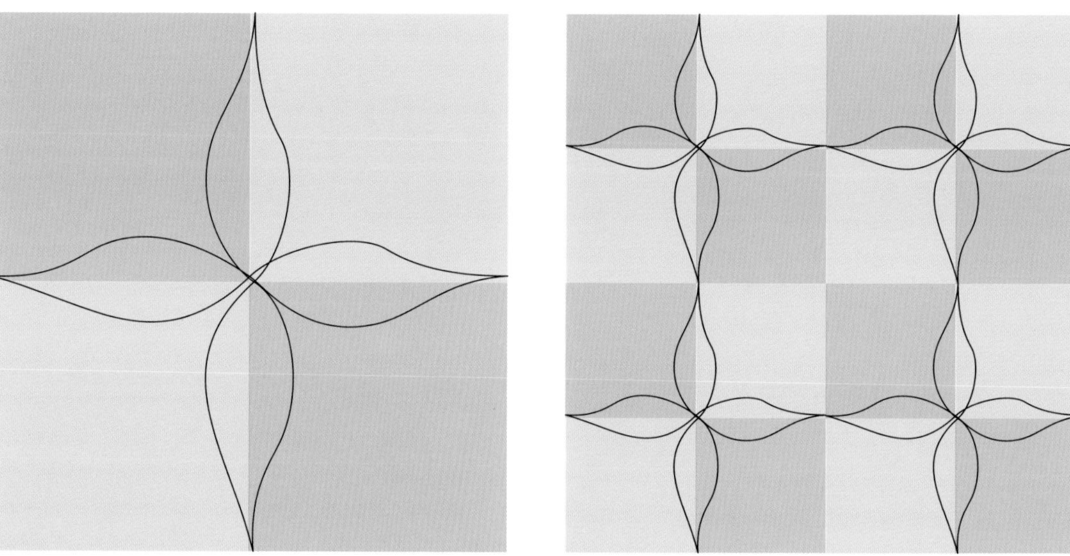

These can be started in the center of the block or at the edge. Just center 4 Sunshine Petals around the block center. If you start on the edge, exit where you came in.

SUNSHINE PETALS + DOUBLE HOOKS

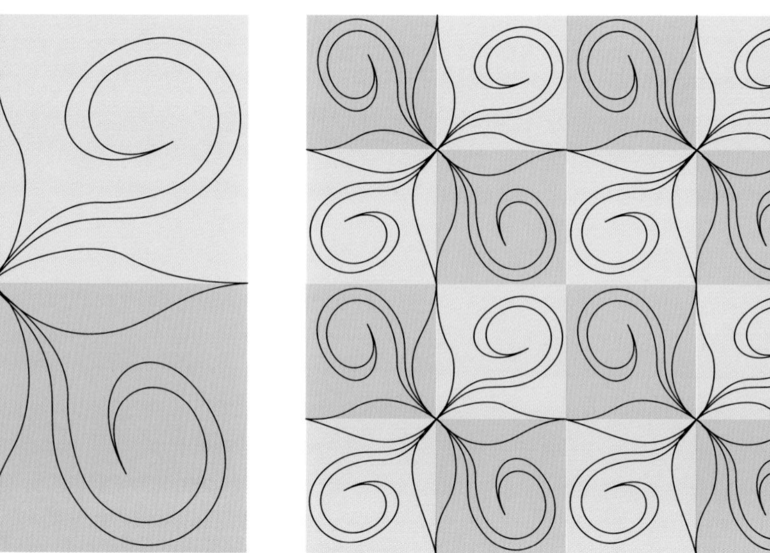

SUNSHINE PETALS + ASTERISKS + STRAIGHT LINES

This works best when you add the Asterisks after the Sunshine Petals are all finished.

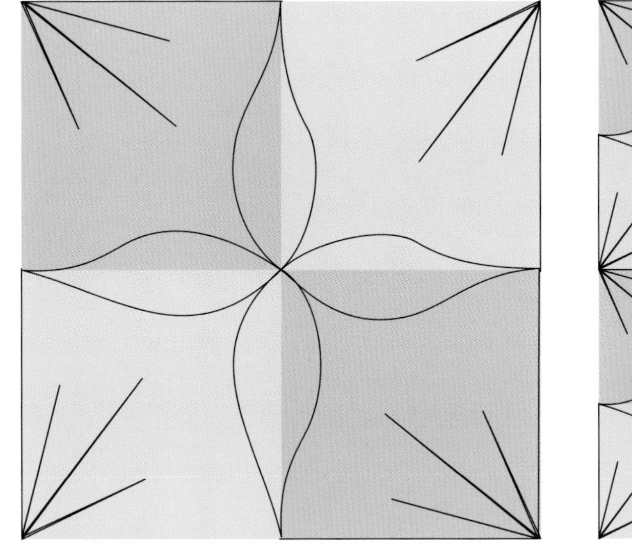

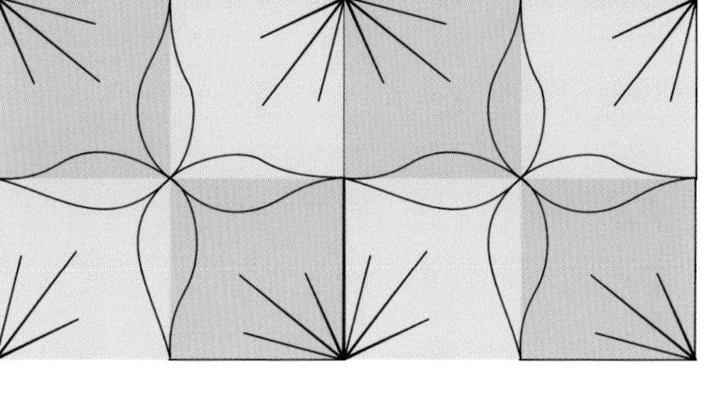

ORANGE PEELS + BUDDED DOUBLE HOOKS

Complete all sides of a square with Orange Peels, then add a Double Hook with a few added sprouts to each one.

ORANGE PEELS + ECHOING + BOOMERANG CIRCLES

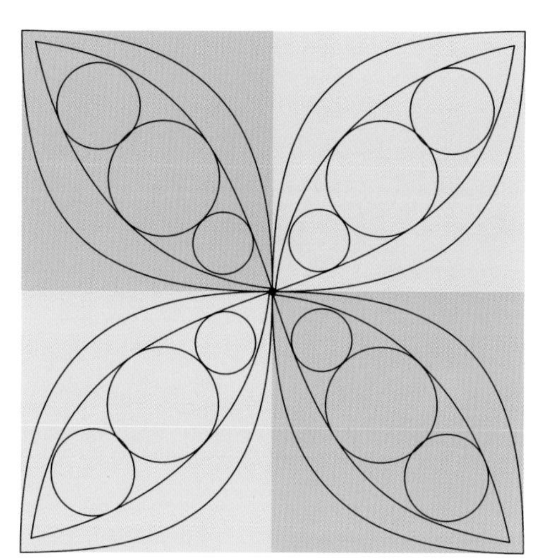

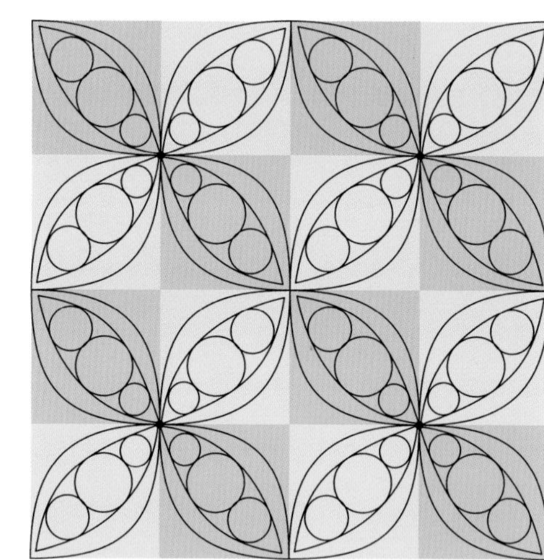

Make a fat Diagonal Orange Peel, an inside echo, then Boomerang Circles to get you back to the block center for the next square.

STRAIGHT LINES + EXCITED WATER

Use narrow tape to mark an X in and a frame around each square. Stitch along the inside of the triangle made by the tape. When it is a closed shape, stitch narrow Excited Water to fill the triangle. Stitch out to the edge of the square diagonally and go into the adjacent triangle shape.

ORANGE PEELS + STRAIGHT LINES + VICTORIAN FEATHERS

Make a Diagonal Orange Peel and echo it. Fill the football shape with grid work that backtracks along the stitched curve. Add Victorian Feathers to the outer Orange Peel.

VICTORIAN FEATHERS + L'S

Feathers from the center out and L's on the way back.

CURVED CROSSHATCHING + ORANGE PEELS + TEARDROPS

Start at the block center and make a curved grid in the solid triangle. Use Orange Peels in the little half-square triangles (HSTs) and add Teardrops at the corner.

BOUNCING CURVES + BOWS

Make bows in this Bow Tie block by putting a circle at the center, and bumpy Teeth Petals with veins. Travel from bow to bow with Bouncing Curves.

ORANGE PEELS + TEARDROPS + DOUBLE HOOKS

Depending on your setting, you should be able to do all the Orange Peels together, then 4 sets of the Teardrop + 2 Double Hook motifs, or spring that unit out of a corner of the Orange Peels.

ROUND SWIRLIES + ORANGE PEEL FOOTBALLS AND DIAMONDS + GREEK KEYS

You will need to stitch along the outside of the block to get from one square to the next.

Half-Square Triangle Blocks and Log Cabins

ORANGE PEELS

FAN-SHAPED VICTORIAN FEATHERS

HEARTS AND CLOVERS (PROPER FEATHERS)

BUDDED SCROLLS + DOUBLE HOOKS

DOUBLE STEMMED FOREST FERNIES

ECHOING ORANGE PEELS + STRAIGHT LINES

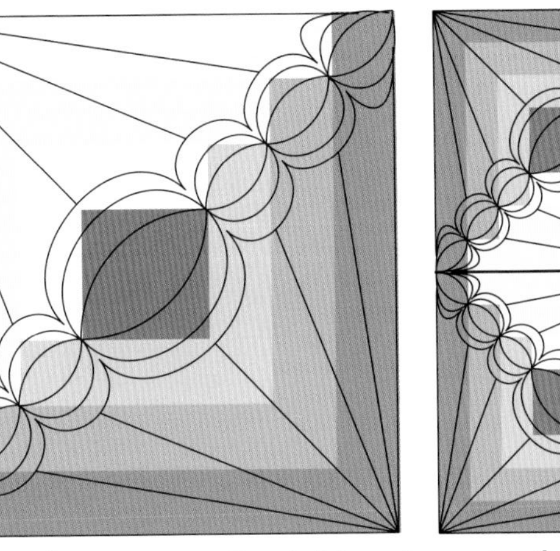
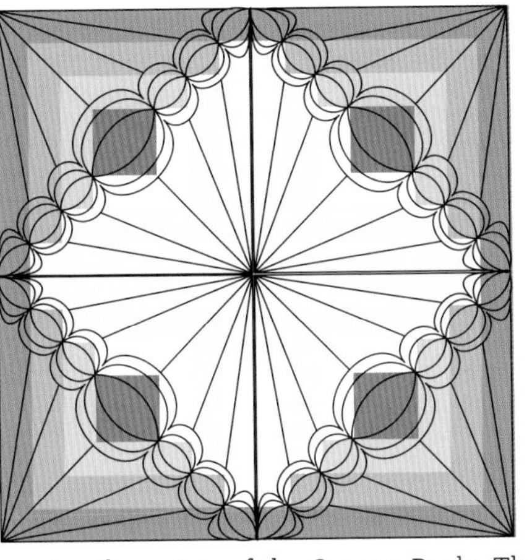
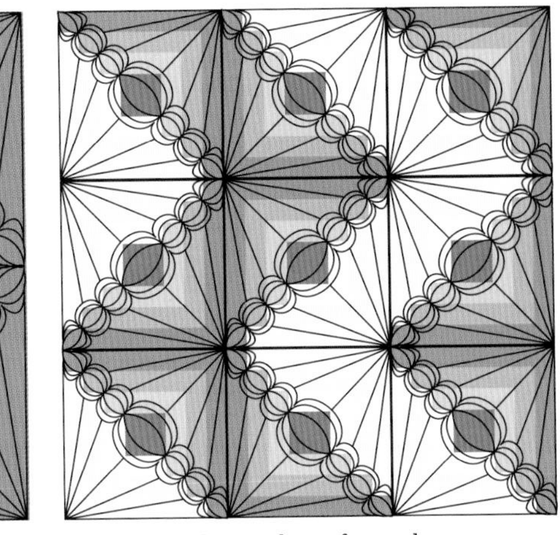

Use the inside corners in a Log Cabin to determine the points of the Orange Peels. Then add lines that radiate from the corner of the block, backstitching along the Orange Peels where necessary.

DIAGONAL ORANGE PEELS + VICTORIAN FEATHERS + ORANGE PEEL FOOTBALLS AND DIAMONDS

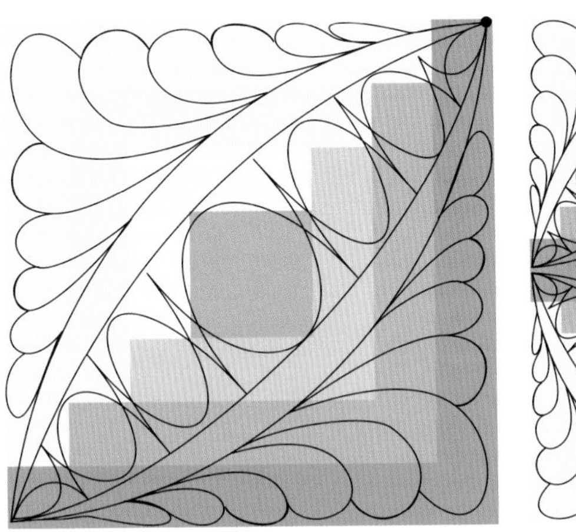

Start with a Diagonal Orange Peel that touches the point of the center square, echo to the outside and use that line for the stem of a Victorian Feather. Make the first Orange Peel on the other side, then fill with the Footballs and Diamonds before finishing with an Orange Peel echo and second Victorian Feather.

Nine-Patch Designs

VARIOUS ORANGE PEELS

Use Orange Peels to make a corner flower, travel through the next square with Orange Peels that meet at the middle of the outside of the block. When you have made a complete round, add Orange Peels to the center square.

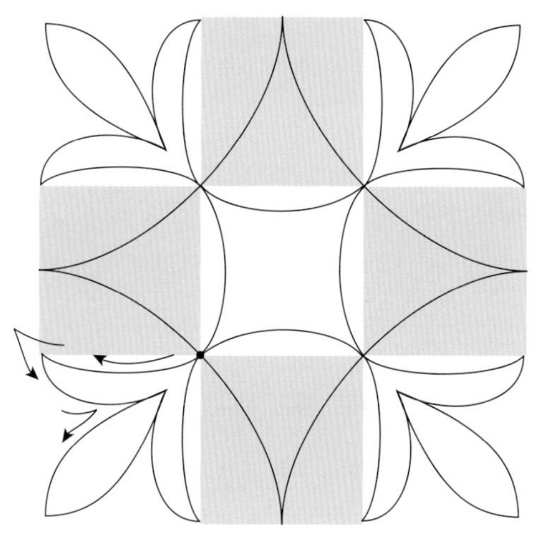

GREEK KEY + KITES + FEATHERS

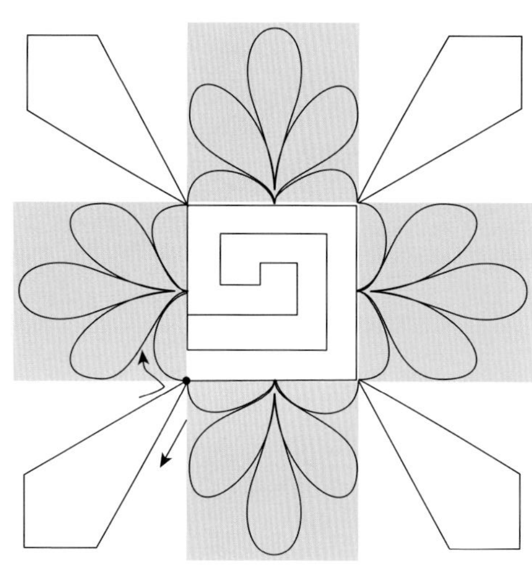

SWIRLIES + POINTED DOUBLE HOOKS

Swirly first, then fill each square with a Pointed Double Hook.

BELLS FROM VARIOUS ORANGE PEELS

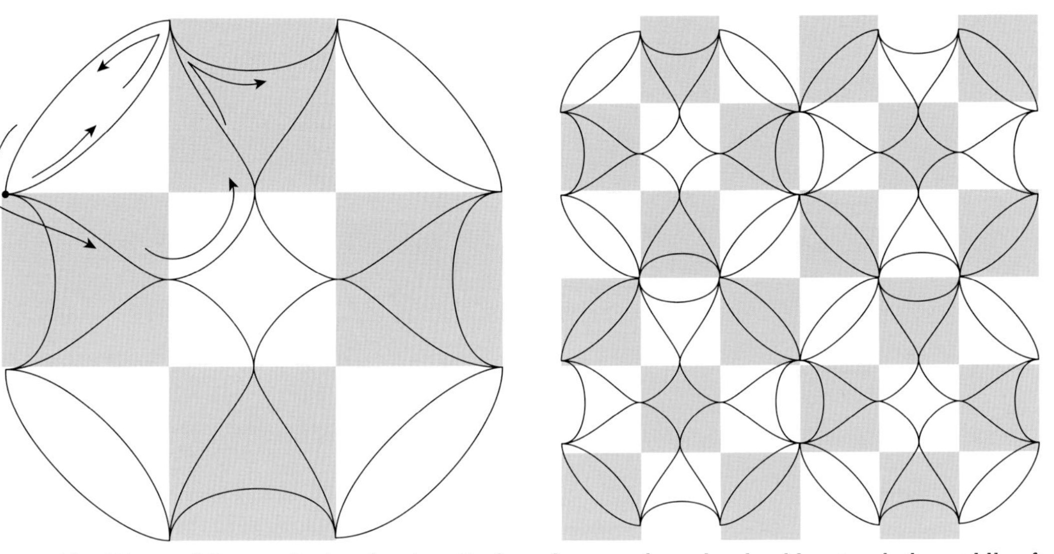

Start with a Diagonal Orange Peel and make a C-shaped curve where the shoulders touch the middle of the center square. Travel to the next with an Orange Peel.

ROSEBUDS + LEAVES + VINES

ORANGE PEELS + STRAIGHT LINES + DOUBLE HOOKS

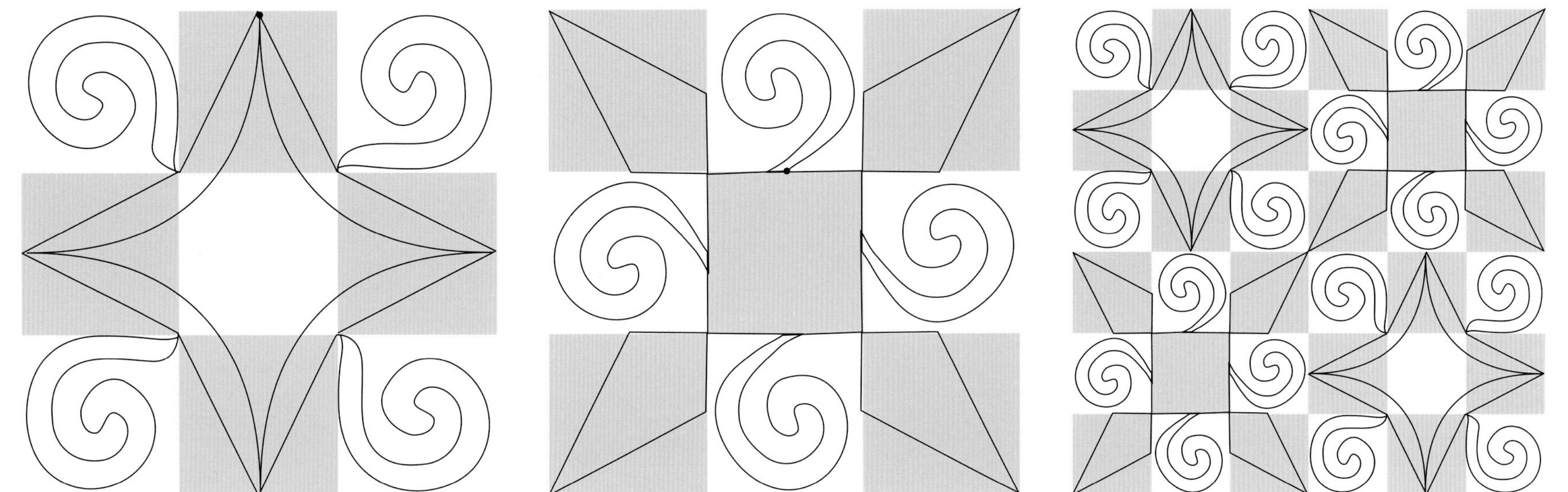

Start with the Orange Peels that begin and end at the middle of the outside of the block. Use a straight line from there to the base of the Double Hook. For the alternate block, stitch-in-the-ditch to about the middle of the seam before making a point at the outside corner.

SWIRLY LEAVES + BUMPY LEAVES

Five-Patch Designs

TEARDROPS + DOUBLE HOOKS + LOOPS

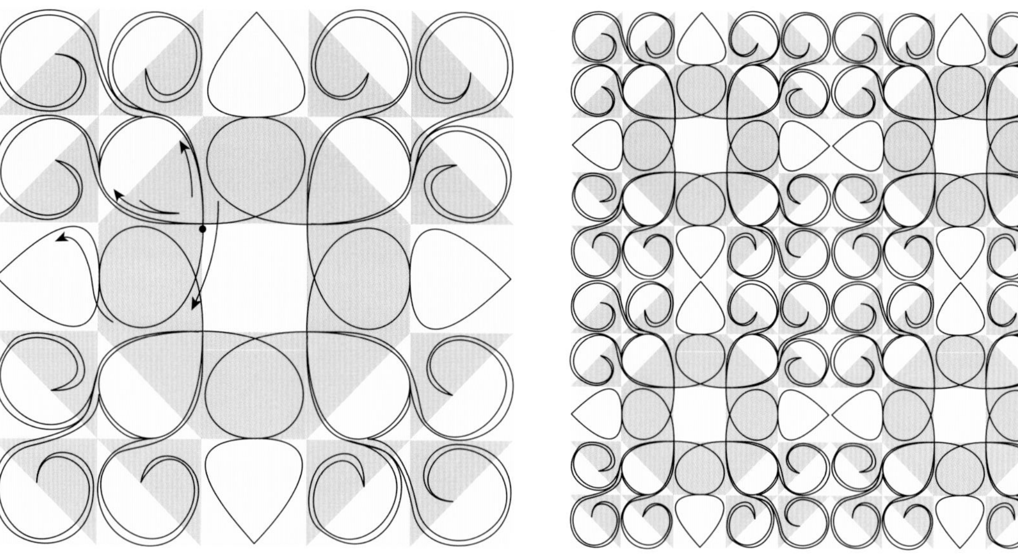

Use a fat Teardrop to fill a square, then backtrack around it while filling 3 more squares with Double Hooks. Travel to the next set of 4 squares with a fat Loop and Teardrop in a figure eight.

TEARDROPS + CURVED SPIKEYS

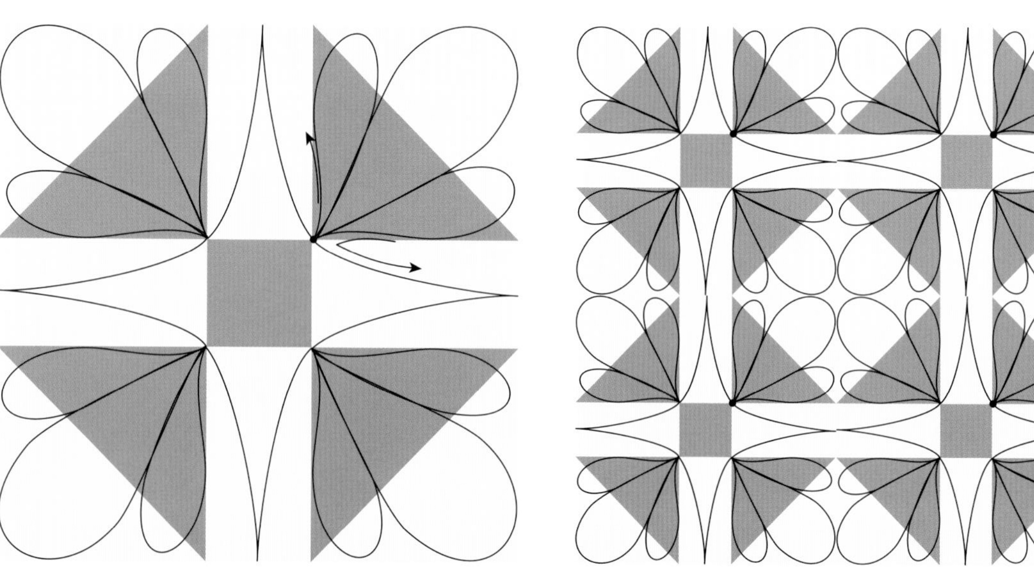

OVERLAPPING ORANGE PEELS + STRAIGHT LINES + TRAVELING CIRCLES

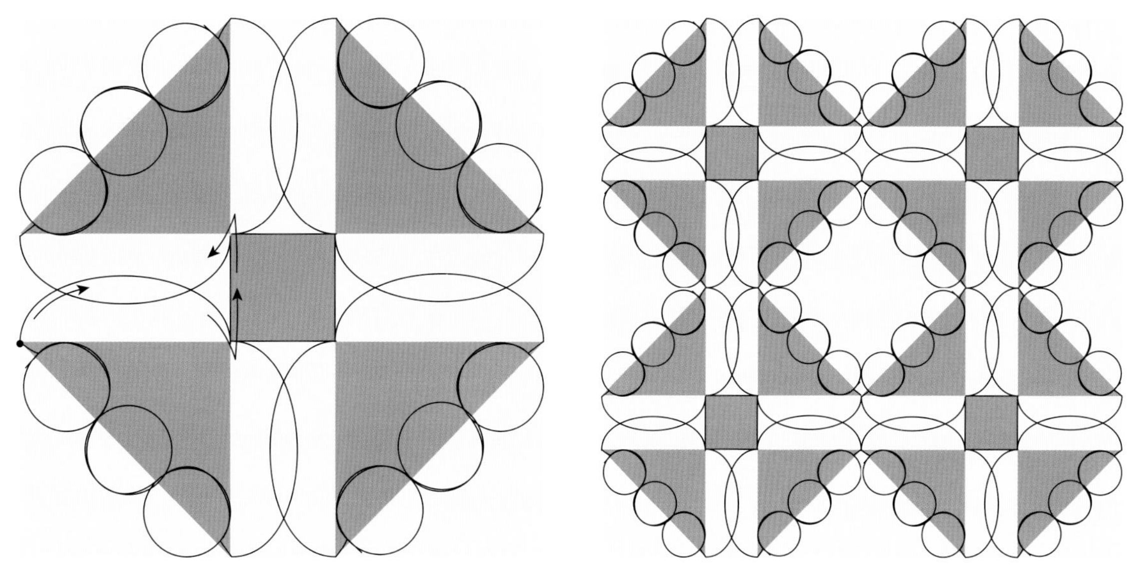

DOUBLE HOOKS + SPIKEYS

VARIOUS ORANGE PEELS + MITERED RIBBONS

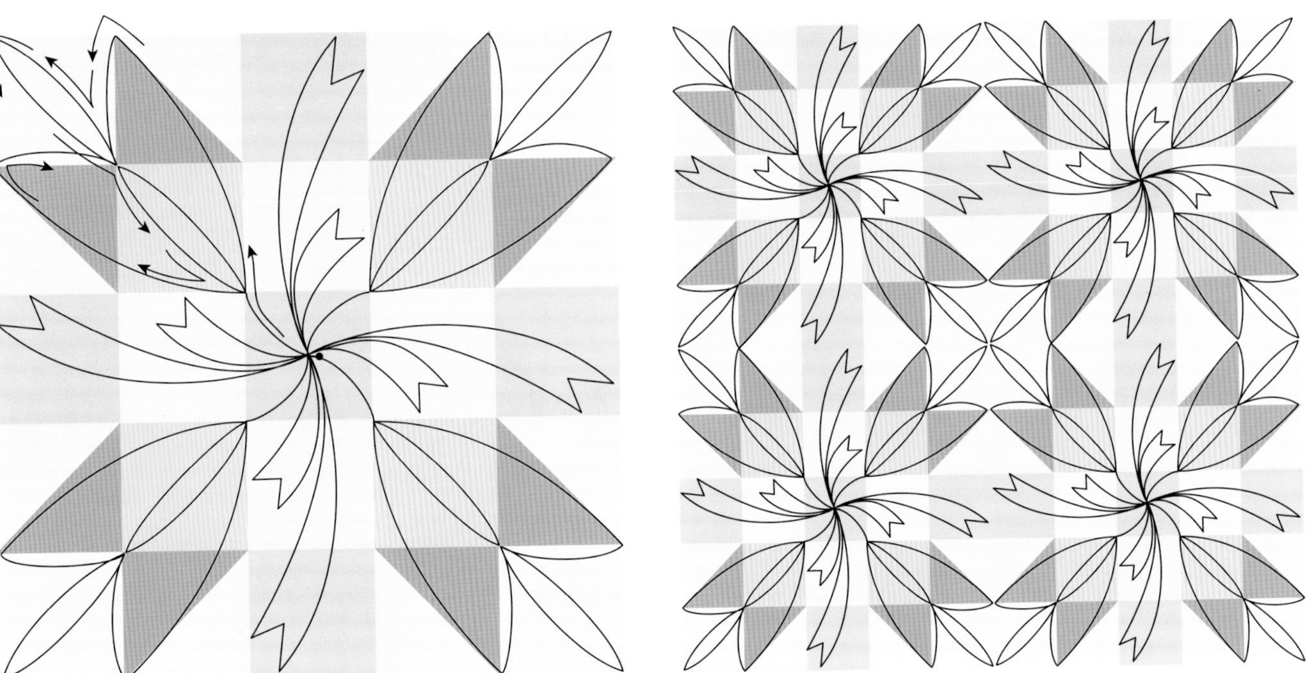

Variable Stars

ORANGE PEEL FOOTBALLS

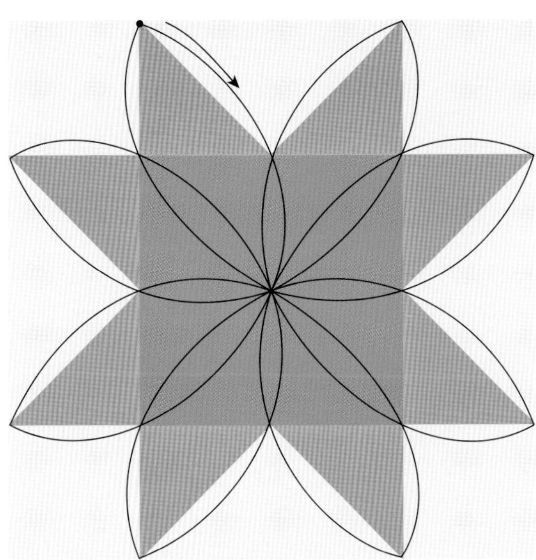

Mark the block center and make an Orange Peel from the outside corner that passes through the point of the triangle. From the center, continue making whole "footballs" all around and finally finishing the second half of the first football.

ORANGE PEELS + FOOTBALLS

Add to the previous design by adding Orange Peels along the inside of the star points.

ORANGE PEELS + FOOTBALLS + TEARDROPS

Similar to the last design, only add a teardrop in the corners as you go.

MORE ORANGE PEELS + FOOTBALLS + TEARDROPS

Add a second set of Orange Peels to the previous designs. This shows you how easy it is to build a motif from really simple shapes!

VARIOUS ORANGE PEELS

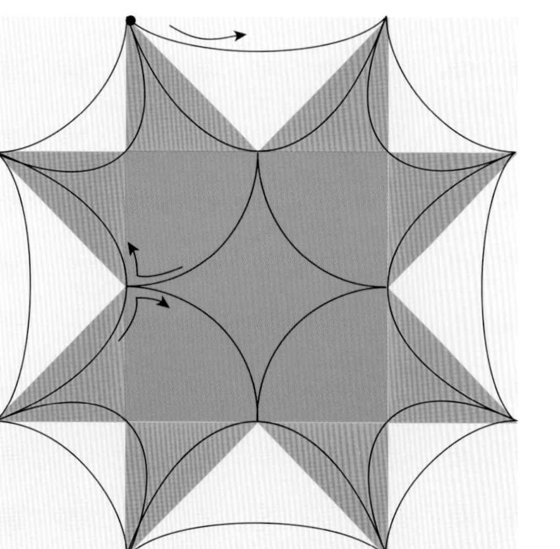

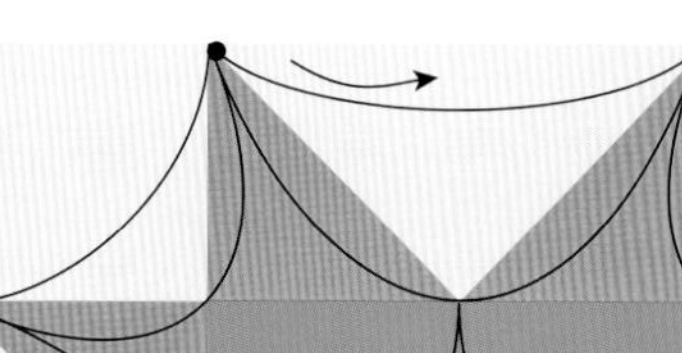

Start with the outside Orange Peels and make another round inside the star points. Before you finish that round, make the center curved diamond.

GREEK KEYS + SCROLLS

This is done in 2 stages—the outside Greek Keys, then the Scrolls emanating from the center.

SUNSHINES + SUNSHINE PETALS

EXCITED WATER GRIDWORK + SCROLLS + MITERED RIBBONS

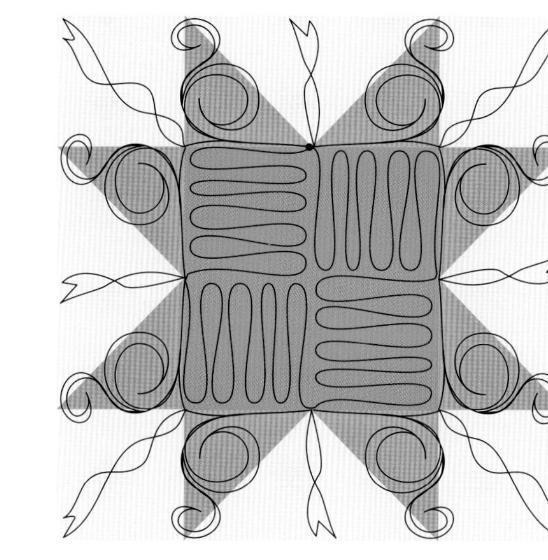

Flying Geese

LOOPS + EXCITED WATER

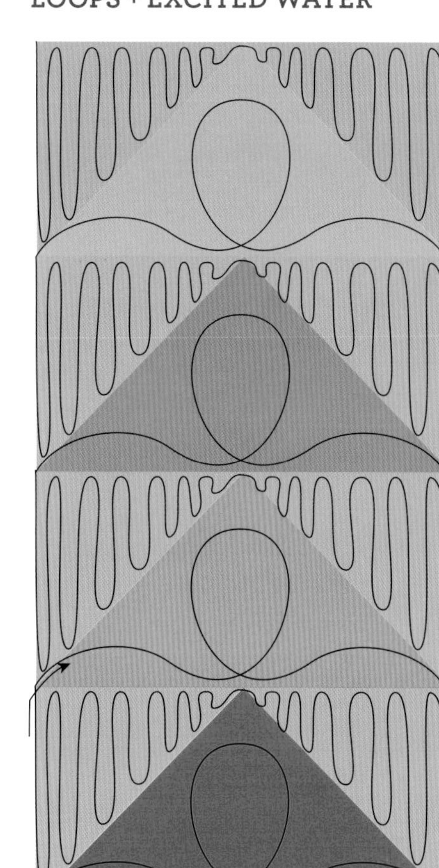

DOUBLE HOOKS + ORANGE PEELS

VICTORIAN FEATHERS + STRAIGHT LINES

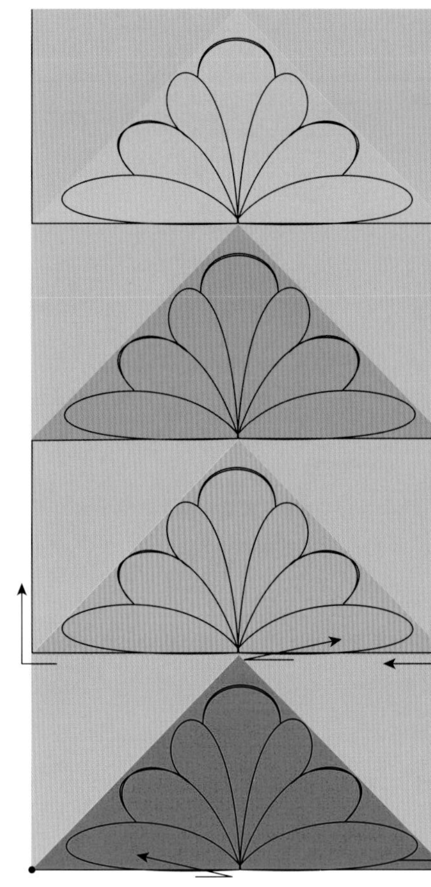

L'S + EXCITED WATER

DOUBLE HOOKS + TEARDROP 1-2-3'S + ORANGE PEELS

Use the Orange Peel to travel to the beginning of the next block, leaving one side open. Finish that last side at the end.

STRAIGHT LINES + SPIKEYS + PEBBLES

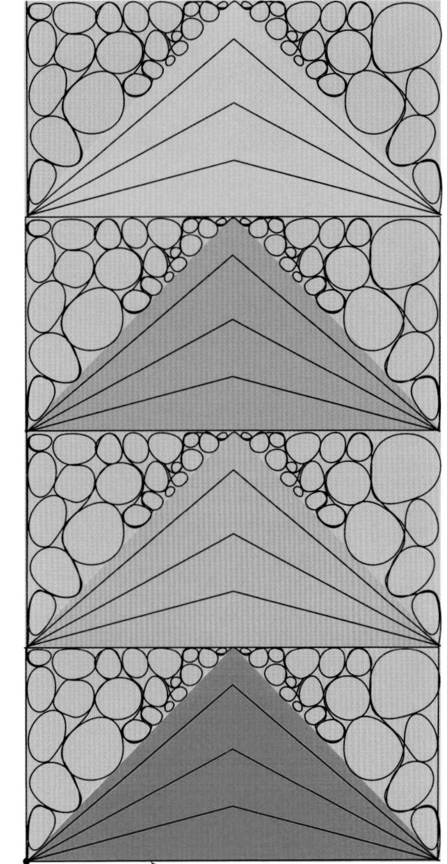

Outline the bottom of the block, then make successively more pointed Spikeys. Fill the outer triangles with pebbles, then stitch-in-the-ditch up the side of the block to the next block.

Priscilla Blocks

STRAIGHT LINES + GREEK KEY

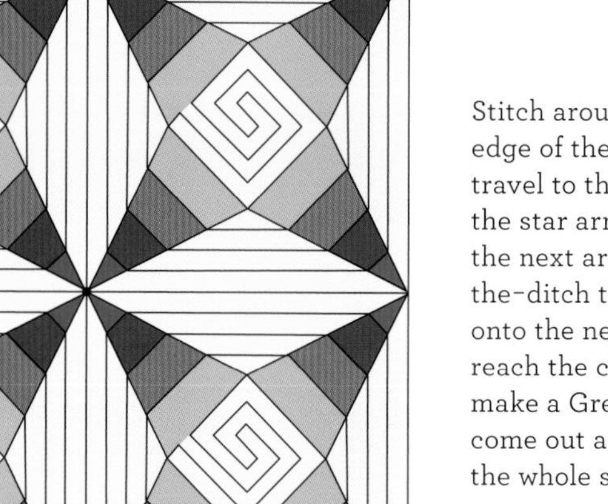

Stitch around the outside edge of the whole block, then travel to the first seam along the star arm. Go straight to the next arm and stitch-in-the-ditch through it, then onto the next. When you reach the center square, make a Greek Key, then come out and stitch around the whole star if you'd like.

ORANGE PEELS + ECHOING + TEARDROPS

After putting Orange Peels around the inside square, add Teardrops in the corners on the second round. Continue to echo, using the cross seams as a guide, and being sure each echo comes back toward the center so the sides of the star are stitched down. On the last one, make an Orange Peel bridge to the next star arm.

TUFTED ZINNIAS + ECHOING + FRILLY LEAVES + LOOPED VINES

Start in the center making the flower, then echo around to make the leaves. Start again to make the vine with a loop in the center.

SPIKEYS + STRAIGHT LINES + ECHOING

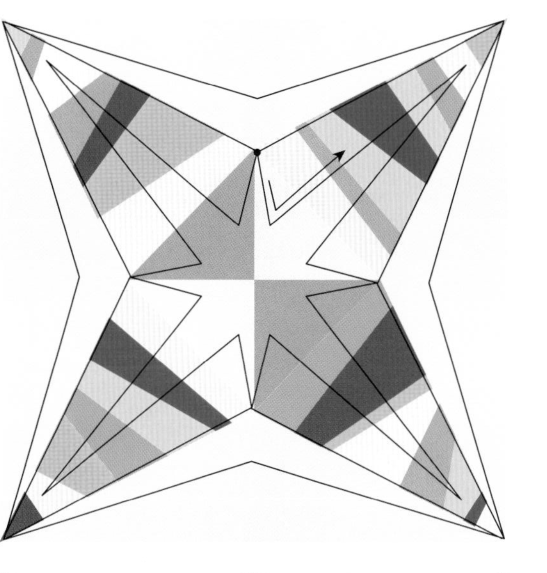

You may want to mark the inside points of the star. When it is done, stitch-in-the-ditch and then echo.

HEARTS + ECHOING + SCROLLS + STRAIGHT LINES

Start in the center with a heart that almost fills the space. Echo half of it and make a Scroll. Come back down that Scroll, finish the Heart Echo, then repeat. Start again to stitch-in-the-ditch and add hearts in the corners.

Snail's Trail Blocks

All these designs follow the "trail" to the middle of the block and continue out on the opposite side. Repeat from the adjacent corner.

EXCITED WATER

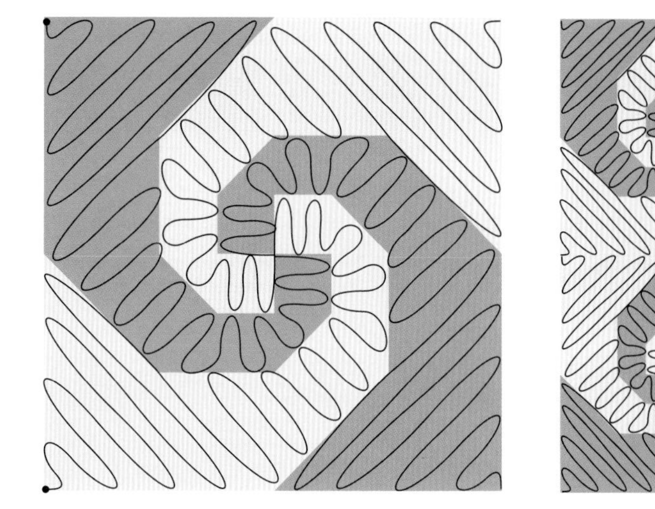

GREEK KEYS

ONE-SIDED PALM FERNIES

RAINBOWS + SCROLLS

Dresden Plates

Dresden plates are stitched out an entire plate at a time before moving on to the areas in between and then to the next plate. Any quarter-circles shown are meant to reveal detail only.

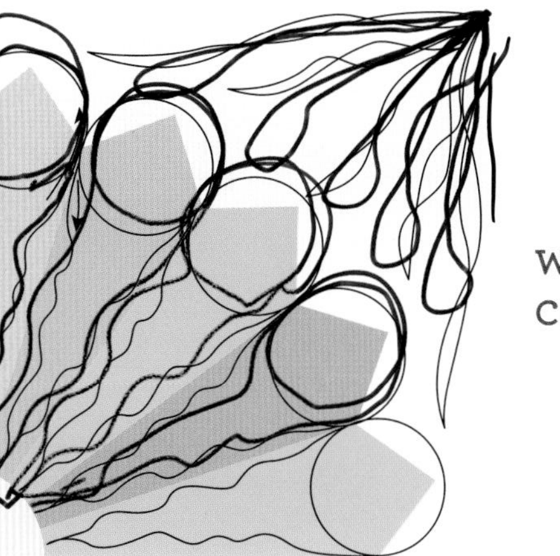

WAVY SUNSHINES + CIRCLES + RIBBONS

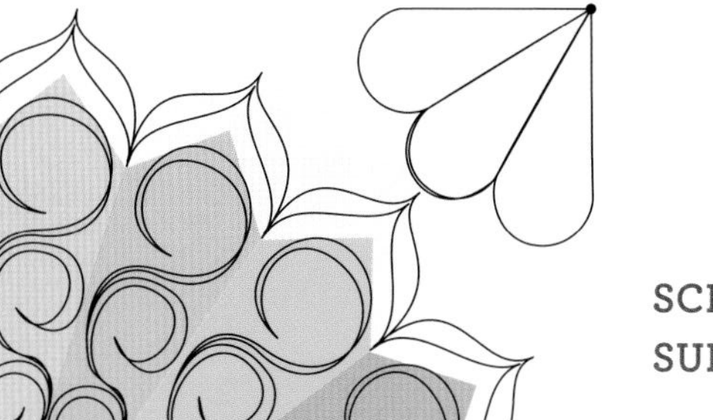

SCROLLS + FAT SUNSHINES + PETALS

New York Beauties and Other Spiky Blocks

RAINBOWS + SPIKEYS + ORANGE PEELS + FEATHERS

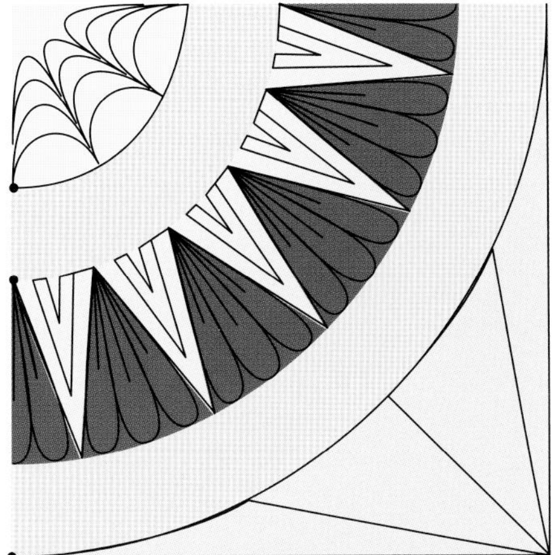

ORANGE PEELS + ECHOING + SPIKEYS + FLOWER PETALS + STRAIGHT LINES

Backtrack along the outer circle while making Straight Lines.

PETALS + SWIRLIES + WAVY SPIKEYS + TEARDROPS + ECHOING

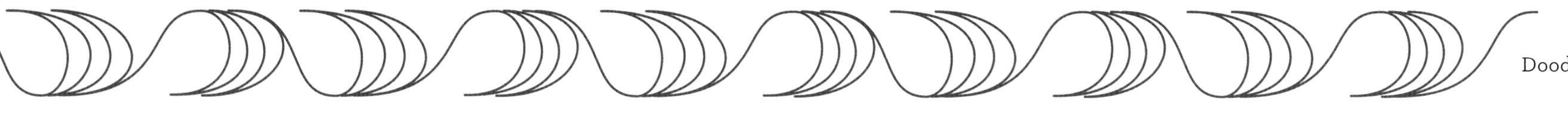

EXCITED WATER + SPIKEYS + ORANGE PEELS

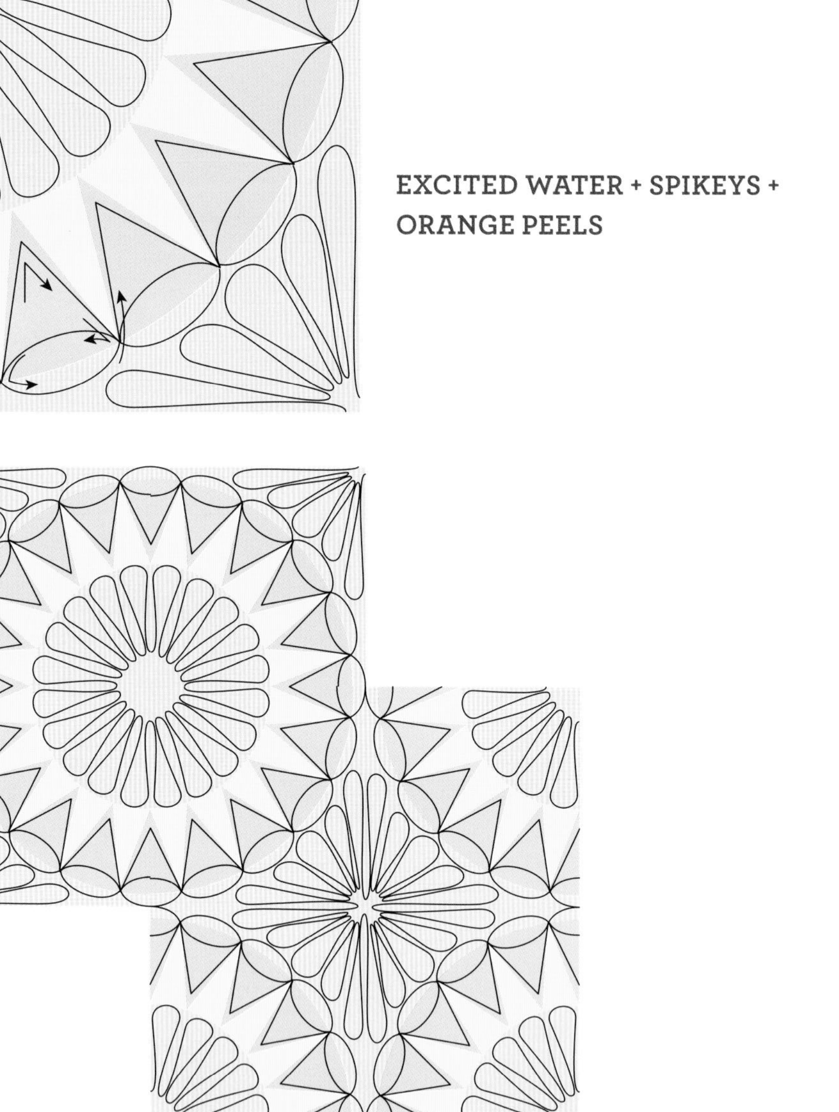

PALM FERNIES + VINES + SCROLLS + SIMPLE LEAVES + ECHOING TEARDROPS

ORANGE PEELS +
STRAIGHT LINES

NO-STEM FEATHERS +
DOUBLE HOOKS +
ORANGE PEELS

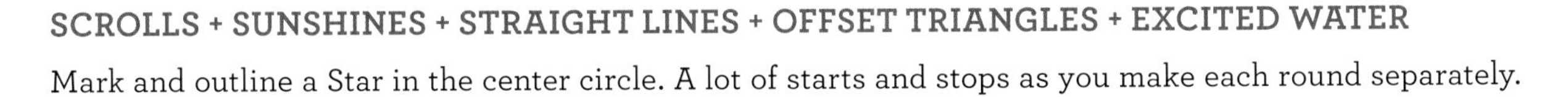

SCROLLS + SUNSHINES + STRAIGHT LINES + OFFSET TRIANGLES + EXCITED WATER

Mark and outline a Star in the center circle. A lot of starts and stops as you make each round separately.

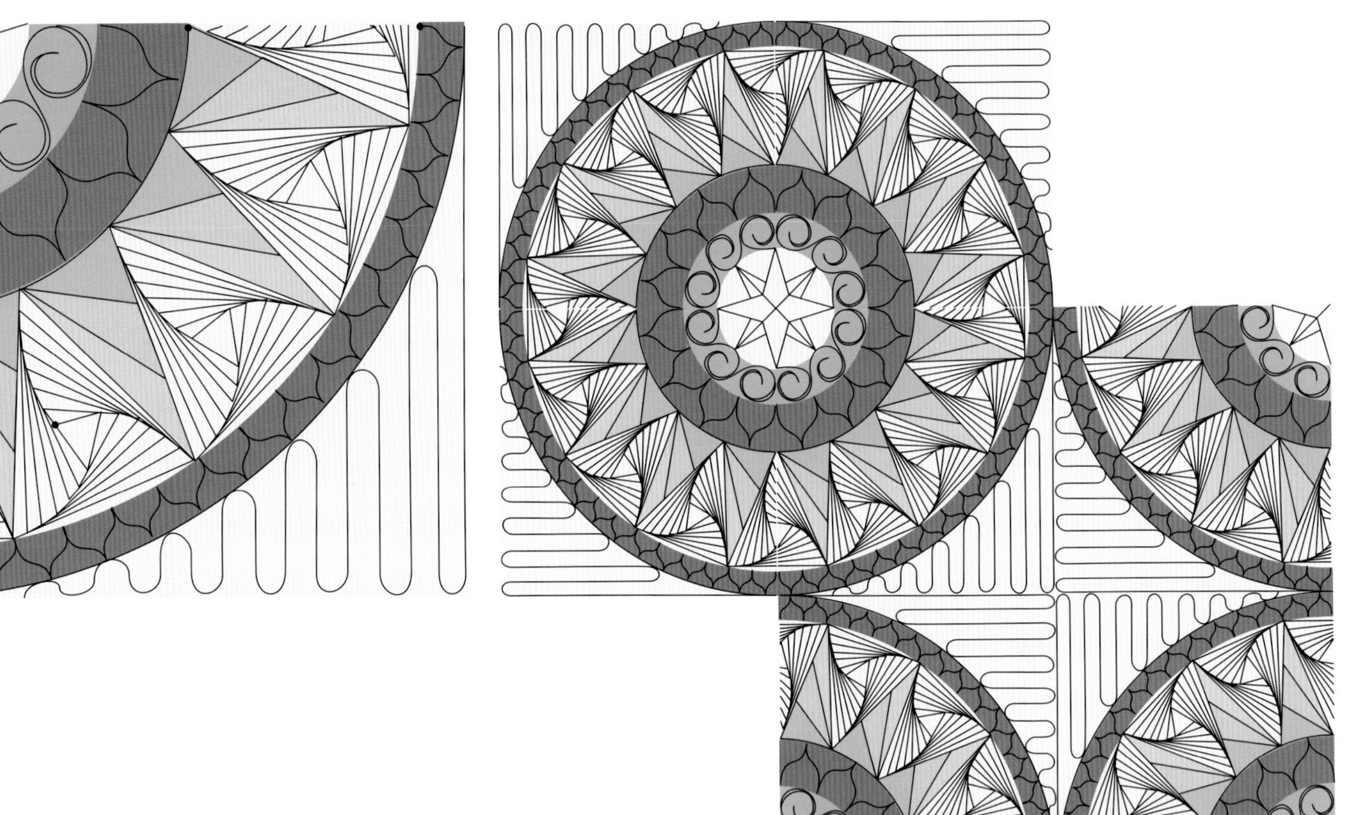

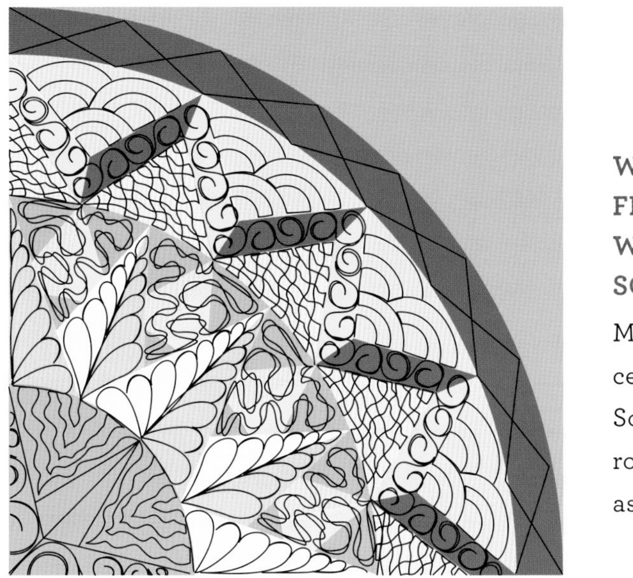

WAVY SUNSHINES + FEATHERS + RIBBONS + WAVY CROSSHATCHING + SCROLLS + RAINBOWS + X'S

Mark and outline a Star in the center circle, then fill it with Scrolls. Work through each round, stopping and starting as needed.

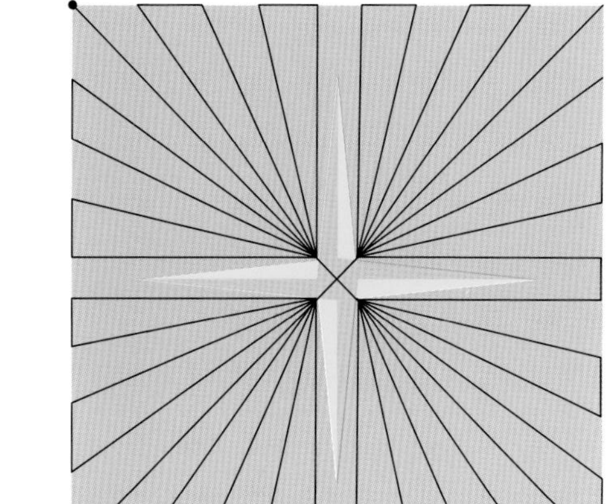

STRAIGHT LINE SIMPLICITY

Ideas for Quilt Layouts

Are you ready for something a little bit different?

Star Settings

SUNSHINES + TRAVELING CIRCLES + STRAIGHT LINES

Divide the space first with doubled Sunshines, then add the traveling Circles and straight, radiating lines that backtrack along the Sunshines.

RAINBOWS + SWIRLIES + FEATHERS

Divide the space first with sets of double Rainbow arcs. Fill the small spaces with Swirlies and the larger ones with Feathers that begin with a Swirl.

STRAIGHT LINES WITH ECHOING + BUDDED SCROLLS + LEAVES + SILLY HALF FLOWERS

Divide the space with double lines to form diamonds, kites, and long arcs. Echo inside as shown. Fill the small diamond, the small kite, and the arcs with Silly Half Flowers; the space in the large kite with Straight Lines; and the background with Budded Scrolls and Leaves.

DOUBLE SUNSHINES + CURVED CROSSHATCHING + FEATHERS + STRAIGHT LINES + SCROLLS + SUNFLOWERS

Divide the space with the double Sunshines. Fill the inside of them with Curved Crosshatching. Put Sunflower in the corner, then Straight Lines filled with Scrolls. Fill the remainder with feathers.

TRIPLE VINES + S-CURVES

Divide the space with Triple Vines and fill in between them with S-Curves that alternate direction.

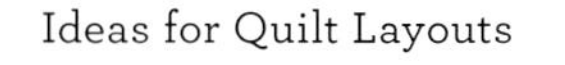

Chain Settings

TEARDROP 1-2-3'S + STRAIGHT LINES

GIANT ORANGE PEELS + SCROLLS

Make the Orange Peels first, then add Scrolls from the center of the Alternate Block.

DIAGONAL ORANGE PEELS + FEATHER WREATHS WITH EYELET EMBELLISHMENT

STRAIGHT LINES + DAISY, LEAF, AND RIBBON WREATHS

ORANGE PEELS + LEAVES + DOUBLE HOOK FLOWERS

Add the Leaves when you get to the outside open square, and then continue with Orange Peels.

Sashing

Narrow spaces don’t have to be boring!

Swirls + Curved Spikeys

Curves that come to a point and bounce from side to side on the sashing.

Curved Spikey Braid

After making the first Curved Spikey, the second stroke of every Spikey should end in the middle of the second stroke of the previous Spikey.

Think out and to the middle, out and to the middle.

Olives

Loop in a Loop + Traveling Circles.

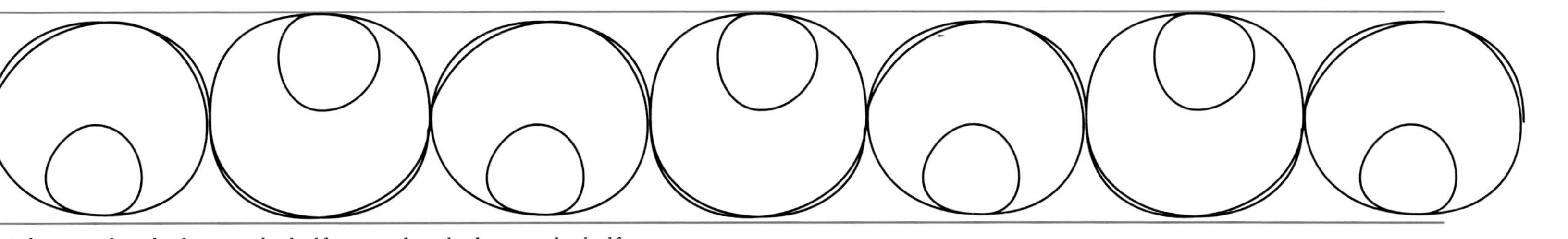

Think around and a loop and a half, around and a loop and a half.

Pineapples

Traveling Egg Shape + Curved Spikey Braid.

Think misshapen circle, around and a half, spike, spike, spike.

Traveling Circles + Traveling Diamonds

This is excellent in an area where there are regularly spaced seams next to the sashing to gauge the size of each element. You will go around and a half every circle and every diamond.

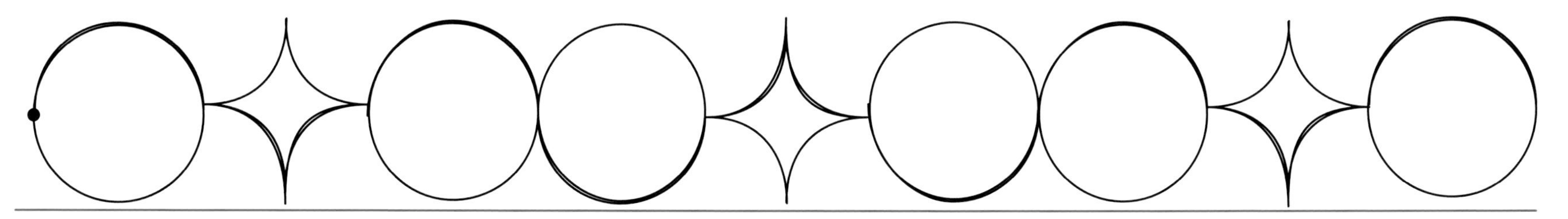

Traveling Ovals + Skinny Traveling Diamonds

How about if we stretch out the circles and squish the diamonds?

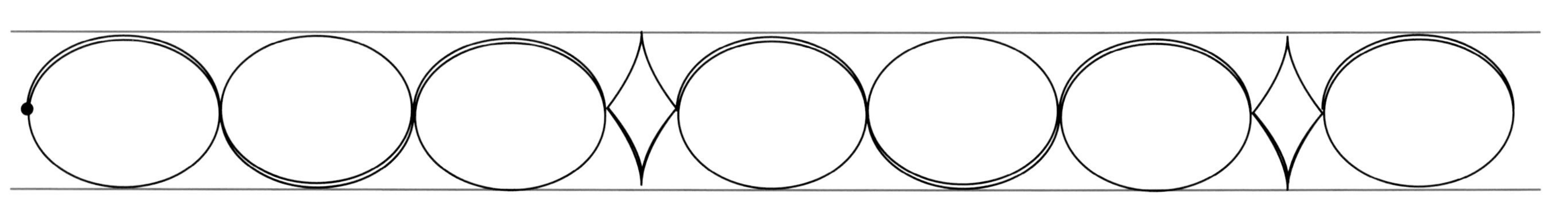

Straight Line X's

This is another design that works well next to regularly spaced seams. Alternately, you could mark at regular intervals.

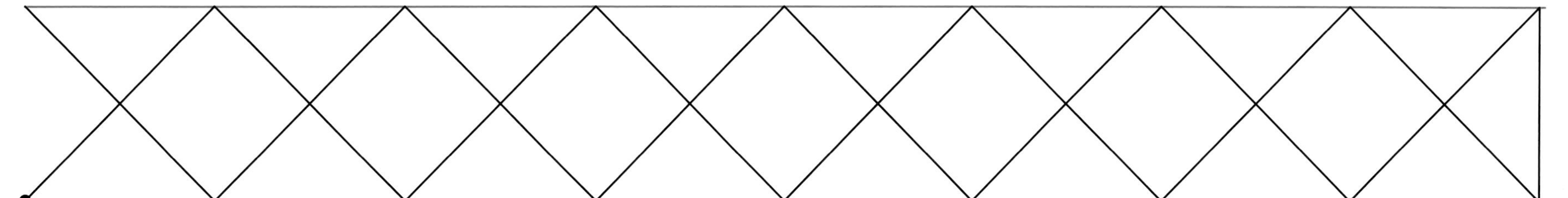

Make a zigzag from one end to the other, then stitch-in-the-ditch to the other side, and return.

Teardrops + Curved Spikeys

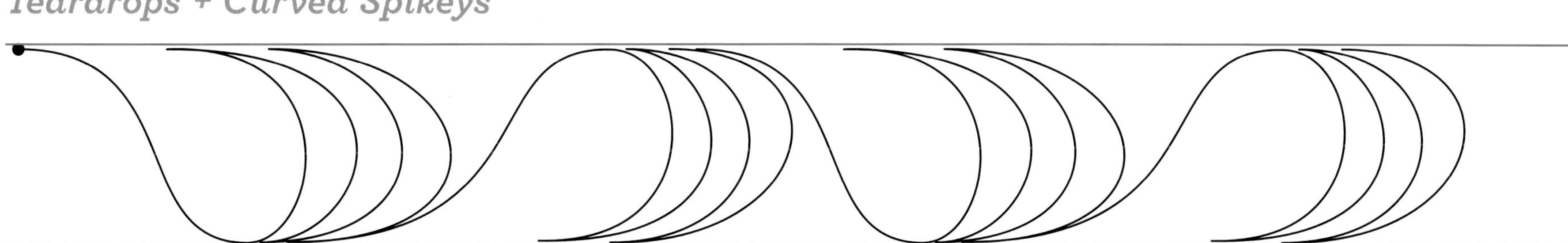

Start with a teardrop as if you were making a feather, but don't quite close it, then echo with Curved Spikeys until you are on the opposite side where you started, then repeat from there.

Orange Peel Footballs and Diamonds

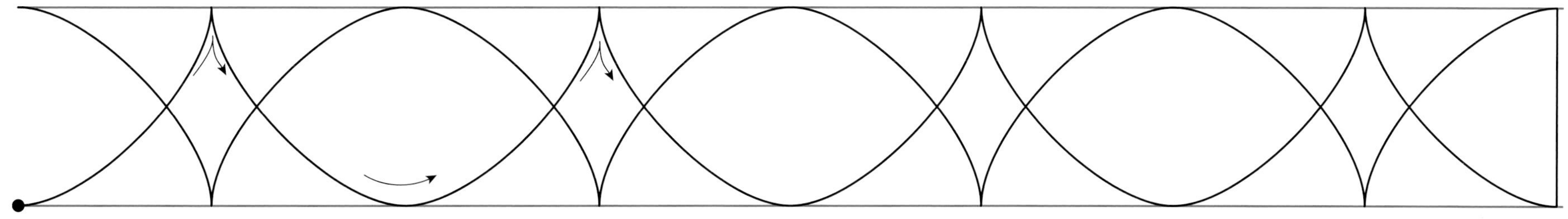

Use seam allowances or chalk to mark a grid of squares in your sash. Then make an Orange Peel that bounces from one side of the sashing to the next. Stitch-in-the-ditch to the other side and repeat going back.

Teardrops + Swirls

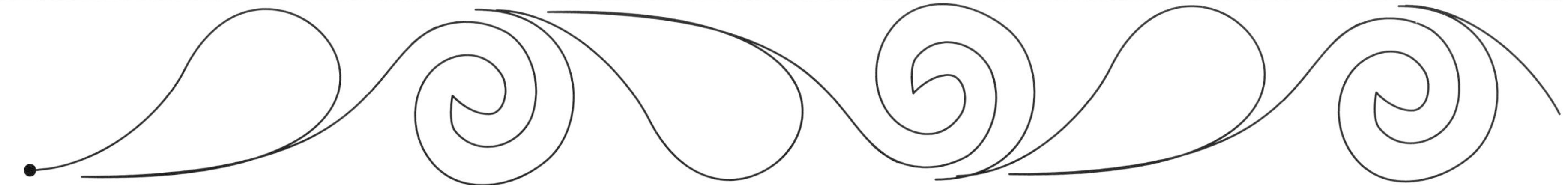

Start your teardrop like a feather on one side, then go to the other side of the sash to start and finish your swirl, then repeat from that side.

Circles + Curved Spikeys + Echoes

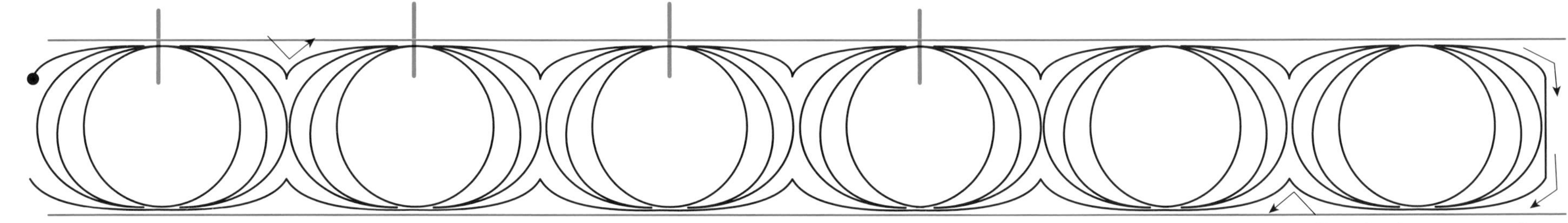

Mark where the center of each circle should be, then make a Curved Spikey, a Circle, a Curved Spikey, then echo part way down, make a point, and reflect that last curve. Make another Curved Spikey, and a Circle, and so on, until you get to the end of the sashing. Echo around to the bottom of the sashing and add the last curved line with points between the circles.

Traveling Circles + S-Curves

This is just 3 Traveling Circles set at an angle with 3 S-Curves in between.

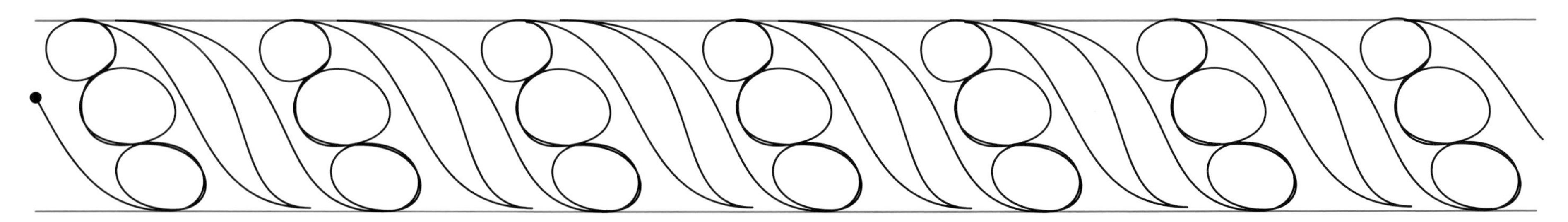

Ping Pong

Start with an angled line on one end of the sashing, then make a very round loop and make a line parallel to the first line to the opposite side, and repeat.

Dragonflies + Loop Vines

Stagger Dragonflies between a looped vine.

Swirl Feather Garland

Make 2 stubby Swirl Feathers side to side and connect them to the next pair with a short vine in the middle.

Double L's

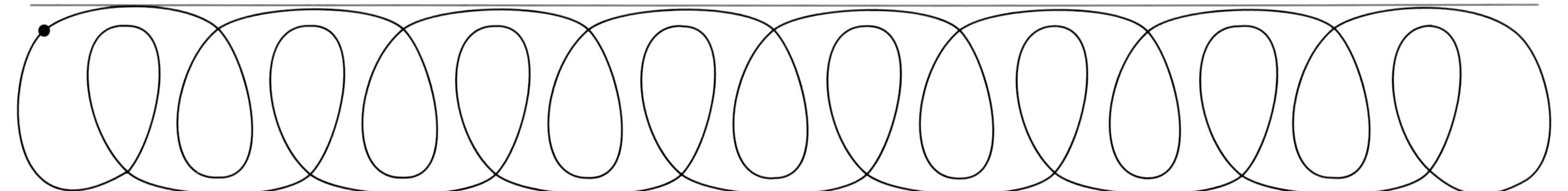

Make lowercase cursive L-loops widely but evenly spaced along one side of the sashing. Then curve around to the opposite side and repeat, putting the L-loops between the previous ones.

Bleeding Hearts + Loop Vines

Start with a Bleeding Heart that points to one end of the sashing, then use a Loop Vine to travel to a Bleeding Heart in the center, which you may have marked; add more Loop Vine to another Bleeding Heart.

S-Curves

Continuous S-Curves that bounce from side to side.

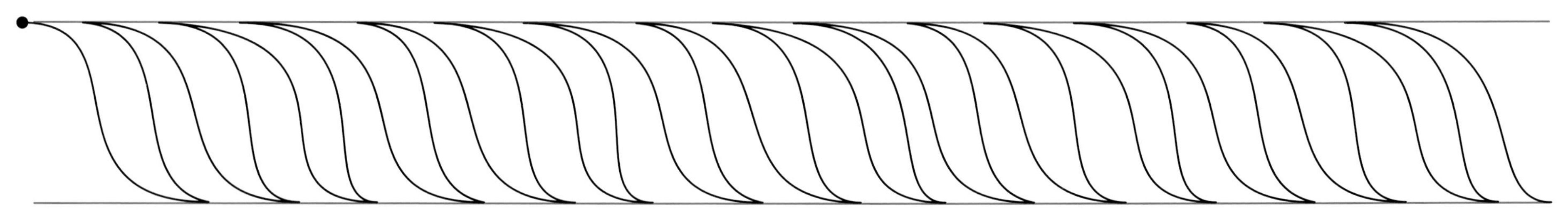

Simple Leaves + Oak Leaves + Ivy Leaves + Vines

Angle various leaves from side to side on the sashing, connecting with a curved Vine.

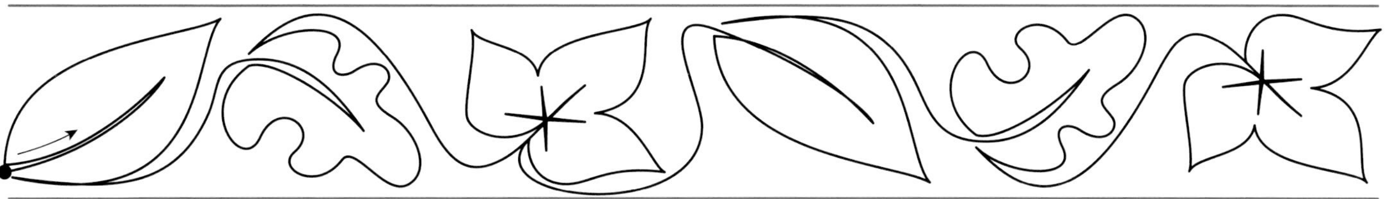

Starry Night Triple Vines + Stars

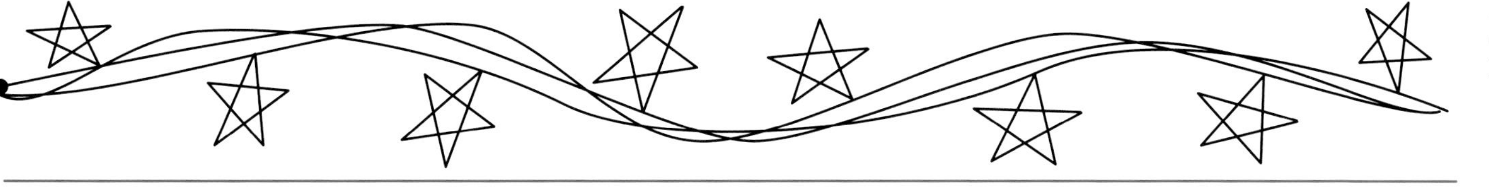

Make a Triple Vine that goes from one end of the sashing to the other. On the last pass, dangle stars from each side.

Continuous Footballs

You may want to mark one end of the footballs. Bounce from one side of the sashing to the other with a curved line that comes to a point when the next one starts. Keep them close together and try to cross at the line you marked.

Continuous Hearts

These are wide-topped cursive L's that come to a point between each one, forming a heart of sorts. You may want to mark a line to keep the loops consistent.

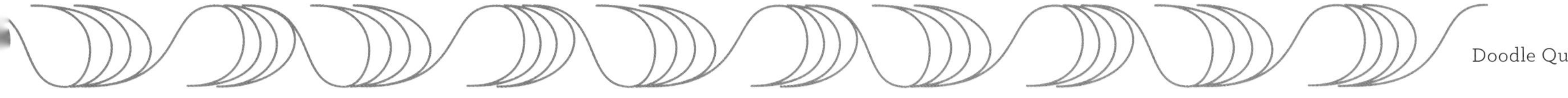

One-Sided Victorian Feathers

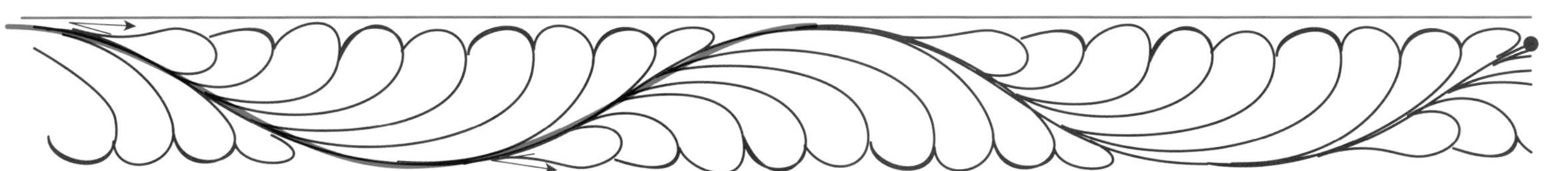

Mark and stitch a curve that nearly touches each side of the sashing. When you get to the end, make Victorian Feathers in the concave part of the curve. Then backtrack to the beginning of the next concave curve on the opposite side of the center line and repeat.

Traveling Bumpy Leaves + Peony Buds

Mark a curve to loosely follow. Along the curve, make the outside of the Bumpy Leaf and when you get back to the starting point, make the center vein along the drawn curve and continue it on into the beginning of the Peony Bud.

Ribbons

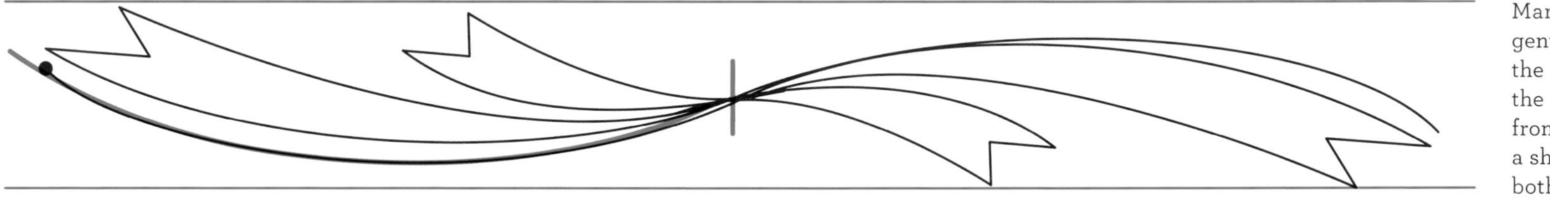

Mark the center, then mark a gentle S-Curve from one end of the sashing to the other. Stitch to the center along the mark, then from the center, make a long and a short miter-ended ribbon in both directions. Continue stitching along the marked curve.

Celebration Sashing

Mark the center and an S-Curve that touches each side of the sashing. Start at the center and stitch a feather with swirls, leaves, commas, and whatever you'd like. Backtrack to the center and repeat on the other end.

Pyramids and Rainbows

Mark a zigzag along the length of the sashing. Stitch the first zigzag, then stitch-in-the-ditch along the edge of the sashing for a bit. Stop and echo the inside of the pyramid twice. Backtrack to the next pyramid and repeat. When you get to the end, stitch-in-the-ditch toward the other side of the sashing and do the same process with rainbows on the opposite side.

Wavy Triangles

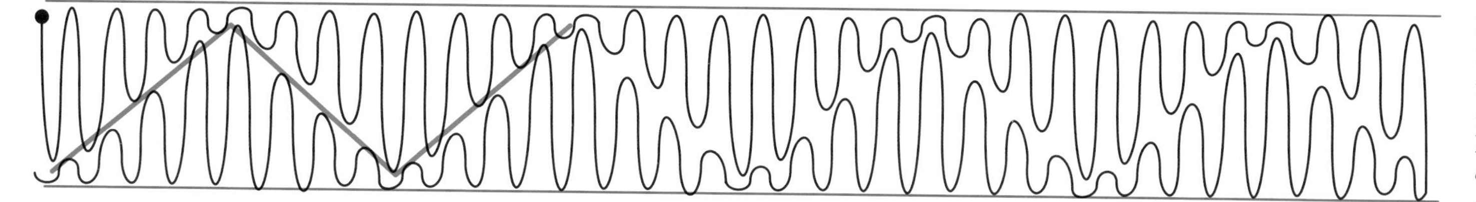

Mark, but *do not stitch*, a long zigzag line from one end of the sashing to the other. Use the edge of the sashing and the zigzag line to determine the length of the Excited Water motif along one side, travel to the opposite side, and repeat until you get back to the beginning.

Triangle Greek Keys

Mark, but *do not stitch*, a long zigzag line from one end of the sashing to the other. Fit Triangle Swirlies into each pyramid from one side, and then the other.

Braided Triangles

Mark a fairly tight zigzag along the length of the sashing. Stitch along the first diagonal, then use the second diagonal line and the side of the sashing as boundaries for echoing that first line up to the point of the triangle. Then stitch along the second diagonal in the zigzag, running over the ends of your echoing, and repeat for the next triangle.

Building a Border

Borders with Continuous Curves

Borders often start with a curved line on which to build the motifs. You can either use your seams as guidelines or use a ruler to chalk in your curve.

CURVES + TEARDROPS BASE

Let's start with a simple curve and Teardrops.

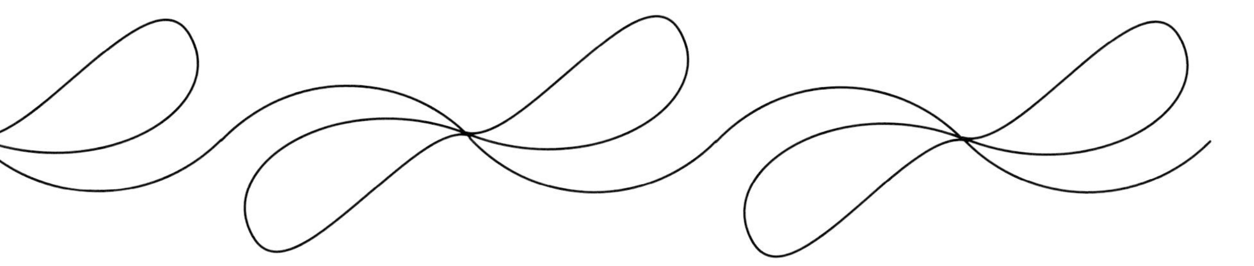

CURVES + TEARDROPS + PETALS + RIBBONS

When you get to the end of the border, come back through with another curve to make a Ribbon.

CURVES + TEARDROPS + TRAVELING CIRCLES

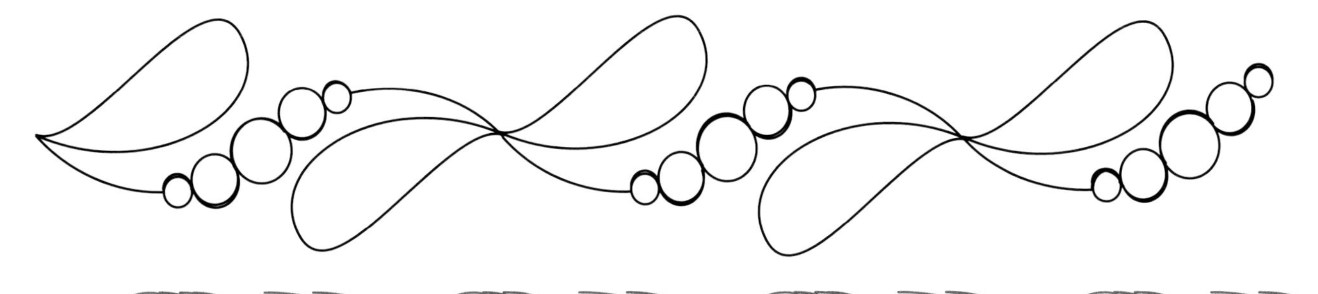

CURVES + TEARDROPS + TRAVELING CIRCLES + COMMAS

CURVES + TEARDROPS + TRAVELING CIRCLES + COMMAS + STRAIGHT LINES

Add Matchstick lines to the bottom that backtrack along the design.

CURVES + TEARDROPS + TRAVELING CIRCLES + COMMAS + ECHOING + STRAIGHT LINES

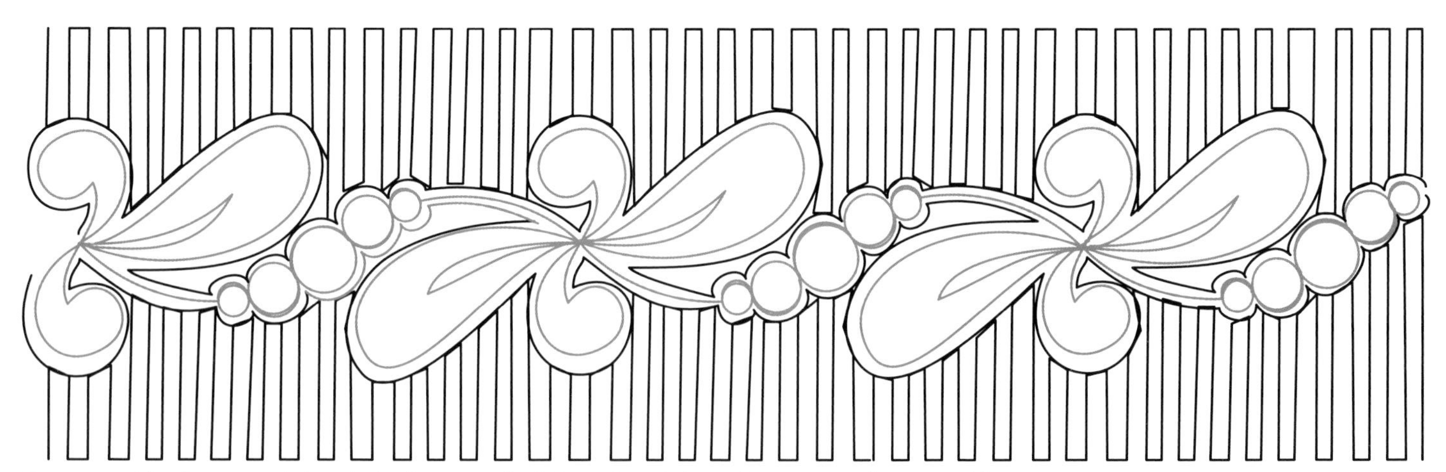

Or you could echo around the whole design and add Matchstick Straight Lines on the top and bottom.

CURVES + STRAIGHT LINES

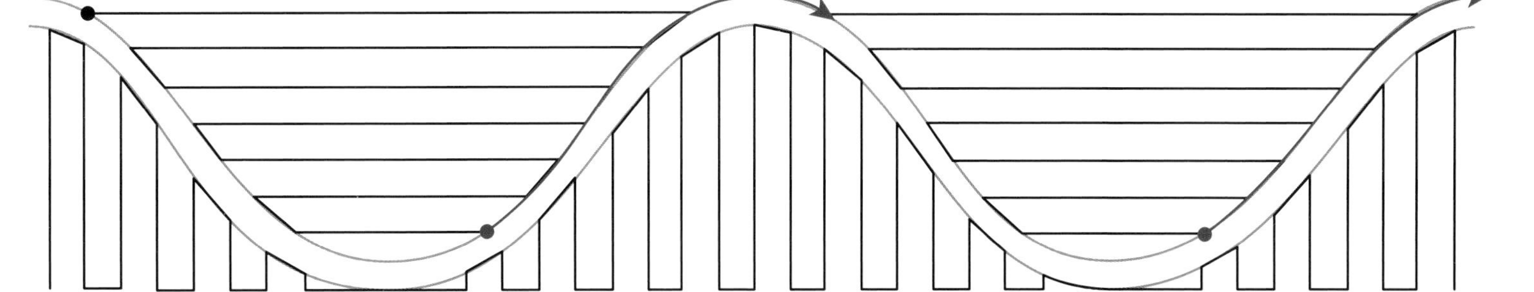

Make your curve (indicated by the gray line) so that it touches one side of your border and is about ¼″ from the other side. Echo that curve ¼″ away so that now there is a curve touching both sides. Add horizontal and vertical parallel lines that backtrack along the curve. Long backtracks are noted by red arrows.

CURVES + STRAIGHT HERRINGBONE LINES

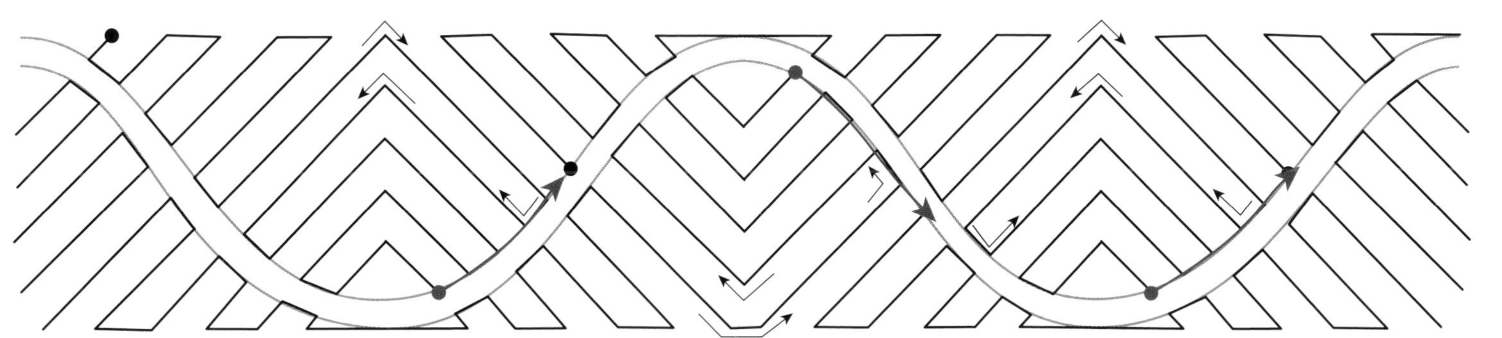

Prepare the curve the same as for the previous design, but change directions at the apex of each curve. Long Backtracks are noted by red arrows.

CURVES + RIBBONS + BUMPY LEAVES

Make the curve, then double back on the curve and add the Ribbons and Leaves.

ONE-SIDED VICTORIAN FEATHERS

Start with the Curve and fill with progressively larger feathers. Backtrack along red arrows.

TRAVELING OVALS + ONE-SIDED VICTORIAN FEATHERS

OVERLAPPING DOUBLE CURVES

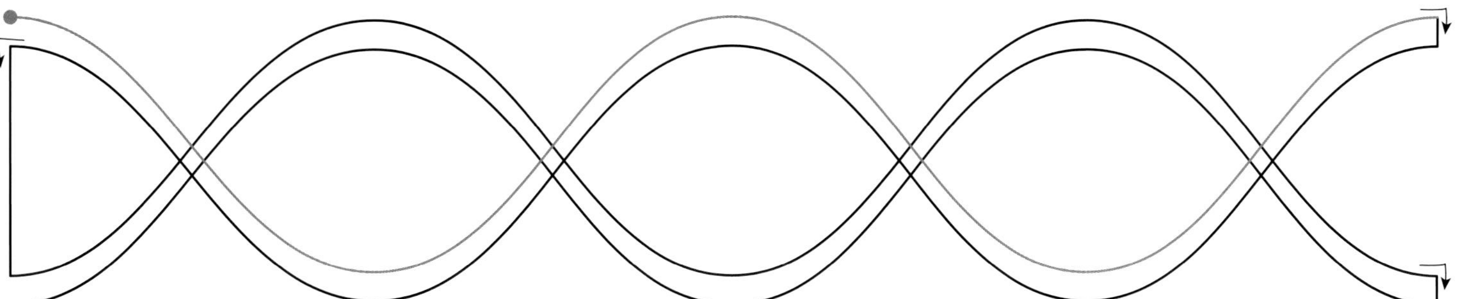

Make your curve (indicated by the gray line) so that it touches one side of your border and is about ¼″ from the other side. Echo that curve ¼″ away so that now there is a curve touching both sides. Travel to the other side of the border and repeat.

OVERLAPPING DOUBLE CURVES + TRAVELING ASTERISKS

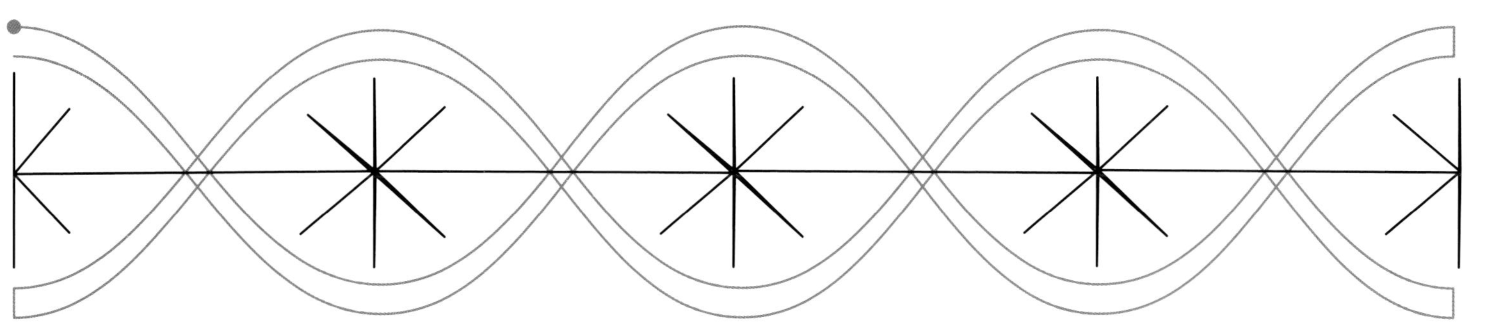

Finish the Overlapping Double Curves and add Asterisks down the center.

OVERLAPPING DOUBLE CURVES + TRAVELING LEAVES + PEONY BUDS

Or add Peony Buds that are connected by leaves where the vein goes all the way through to the next motif.

OFFSET OVERLAPPING DOUBLE CURVES

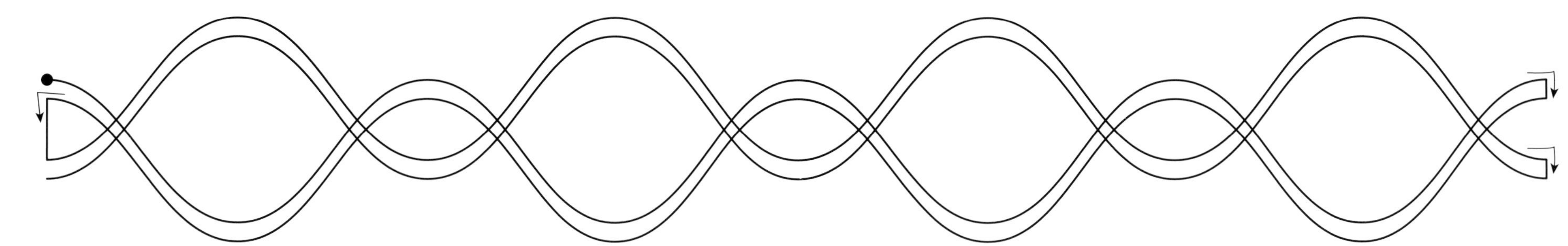

Make these like the regular Overlapping Double Curves, but make the curves go only about two-thirds of the width of the border. They will make an interesting chain.

TWO SETS OF DOUBLE CURVES

If you make the Double Curves half the width of the border and make 2 sets, it makes lemons!

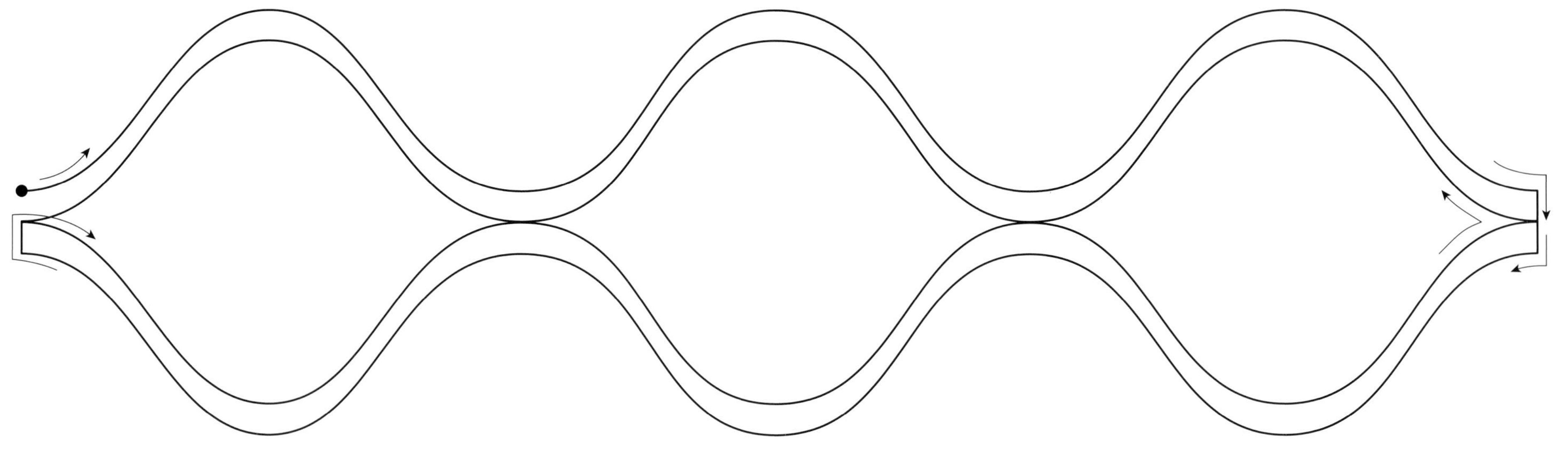

CURVY CAT EYES

Make a Curve that has pretty steep sides and reverse to mirror back to the start. Continue with a narrower curve to make cat eyes.

CURVES + DOUBLE HOOKS

Start with the Curve from the far end and come back up the spine with Double Hooks that fill the space.

CURVES + POINTED DOUBLE HOOKS

CURVES + SWIRLIES + CURVED SPIKEYS

Place a curve that runs through the middle of the border. Add a Swirly with a Curved Spikey on either side of it in each dip.

CURVED FEATHERS

This curve works itself out. Use seams or marks to determine the size of each curved section.

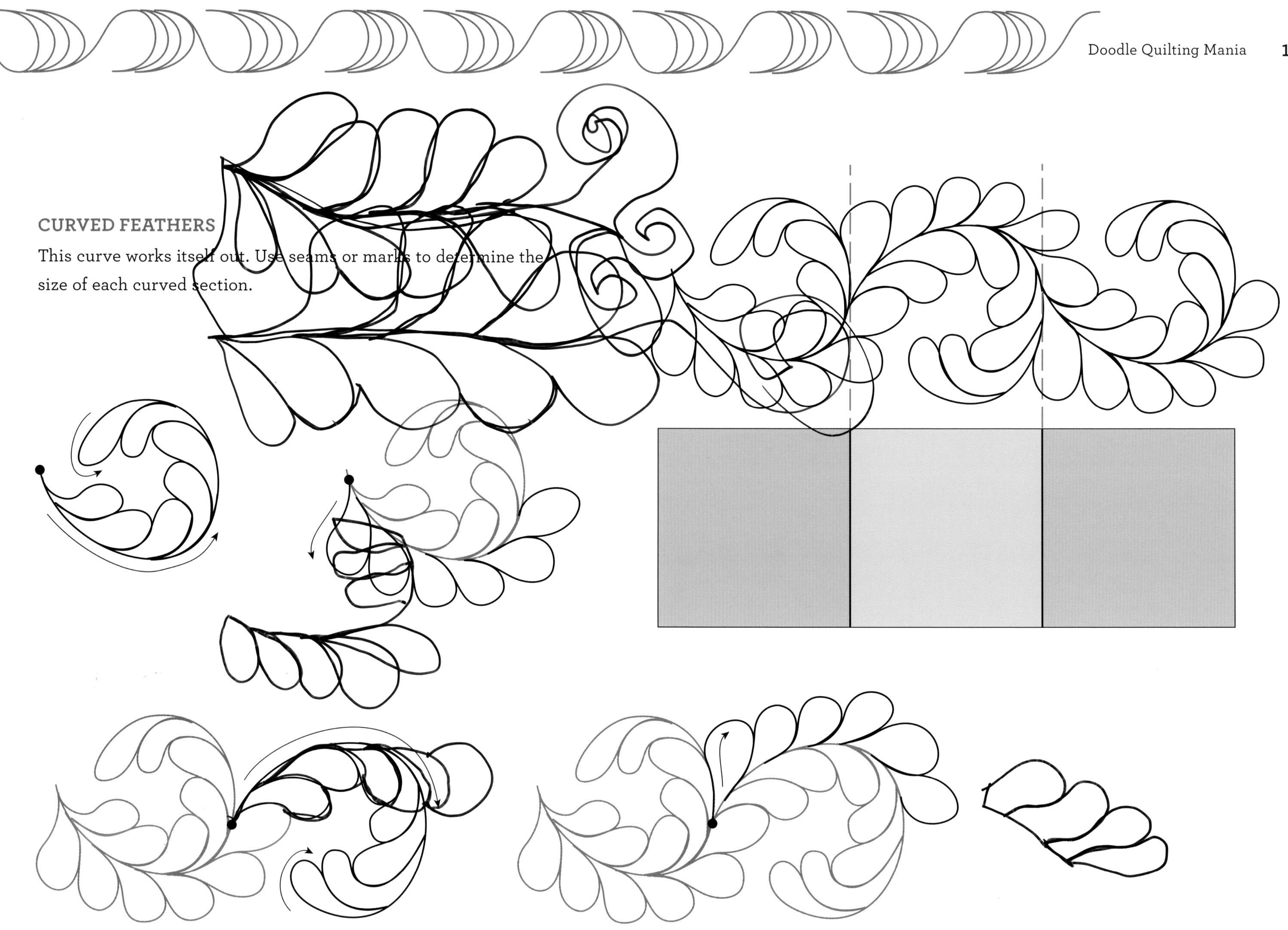

Borders without Continuous Curves

DOUBLE HOOKS + FEATHERS GARLAND

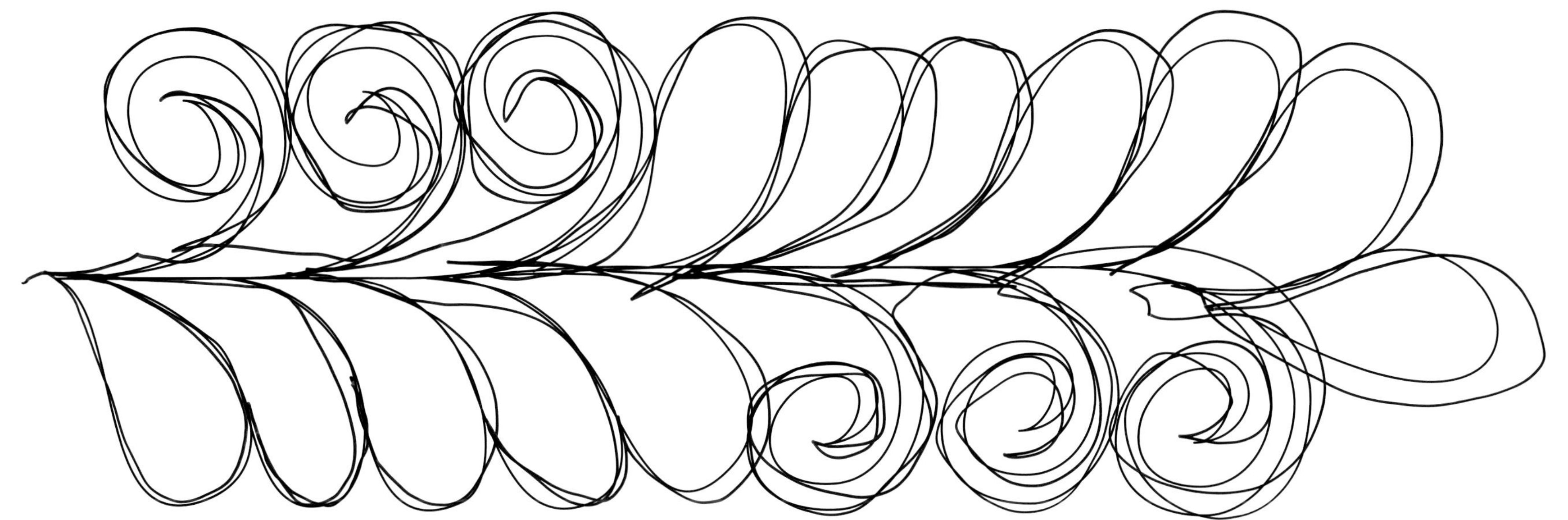

Make 3 Double Hooks that reach all the way back to the beginning, then feathers up the opposite side. Repeat, switching sides.

SCALLOPS + ONE-SIDED VICTORIAN FEATHERS + STRAIGHT LINES

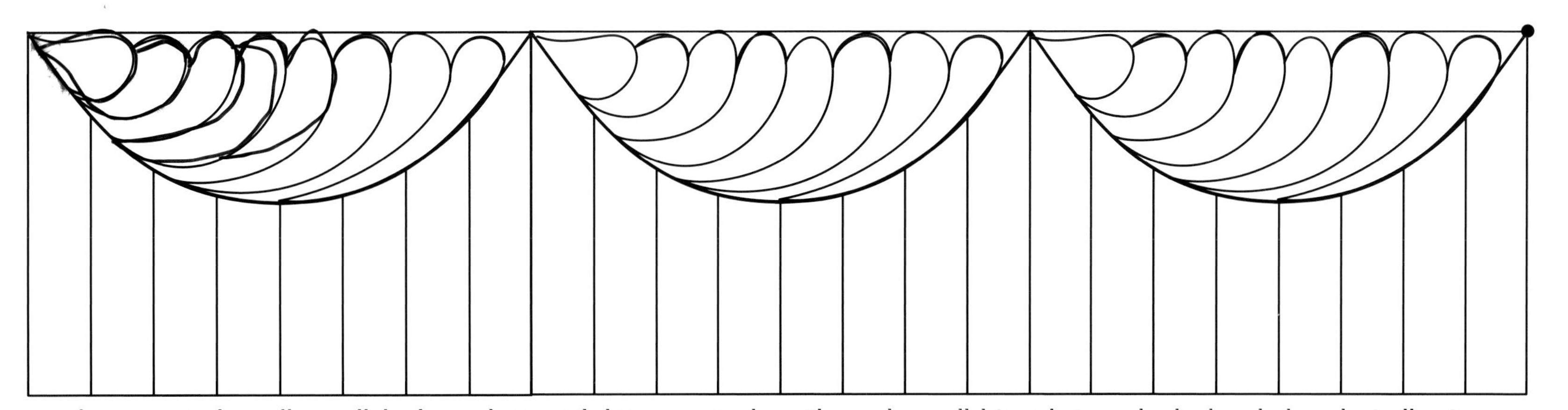

Start by putting in the Scallops. Fill the dips with One-Sided Victorian Feathers. Then make parallel Straight Lines that backtrack along the Scallop Curve.

RIBBONS + STRAWBERRIES

Connect Strawberries with a vine and when you get to the end, go back over the vine to make a Ribbon. Or make two passes, one in red for the Strawberries and one in green for the tops.

CHRISTMAS TREES + LOOPED VINES + HOLLY + STARS

LINES + BOOMERANG CIRCLES

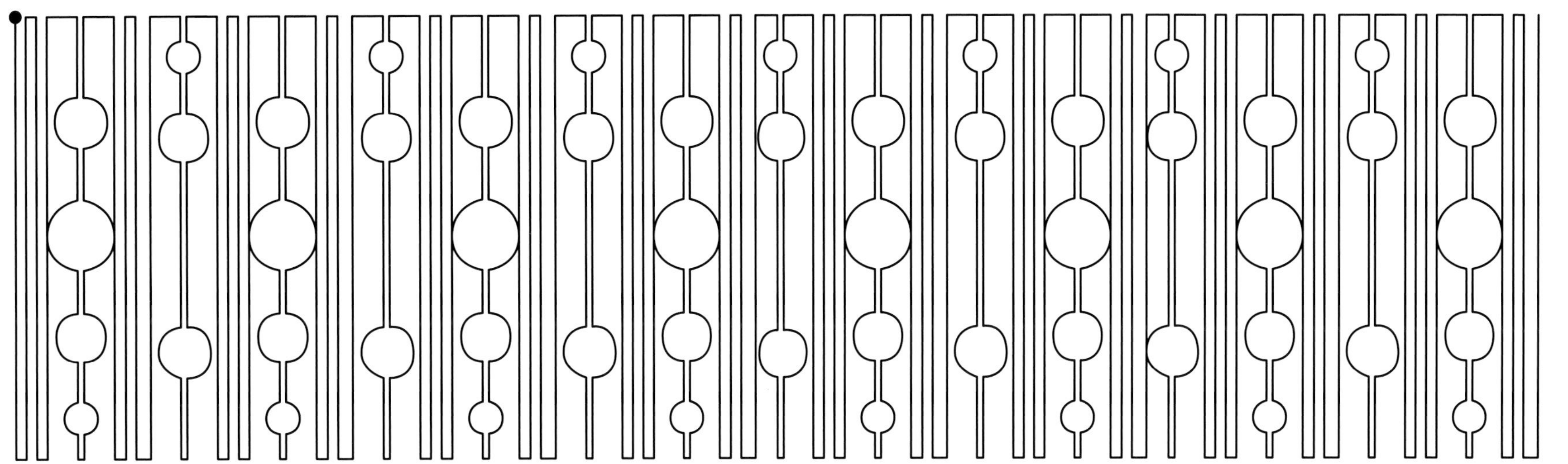

Make parallel lines across the width of the border, occasionally making a wider gap and adding Boomerang Circles going one way; then on the next line, finish them, but don't quite close them.

LOTS OF LINES

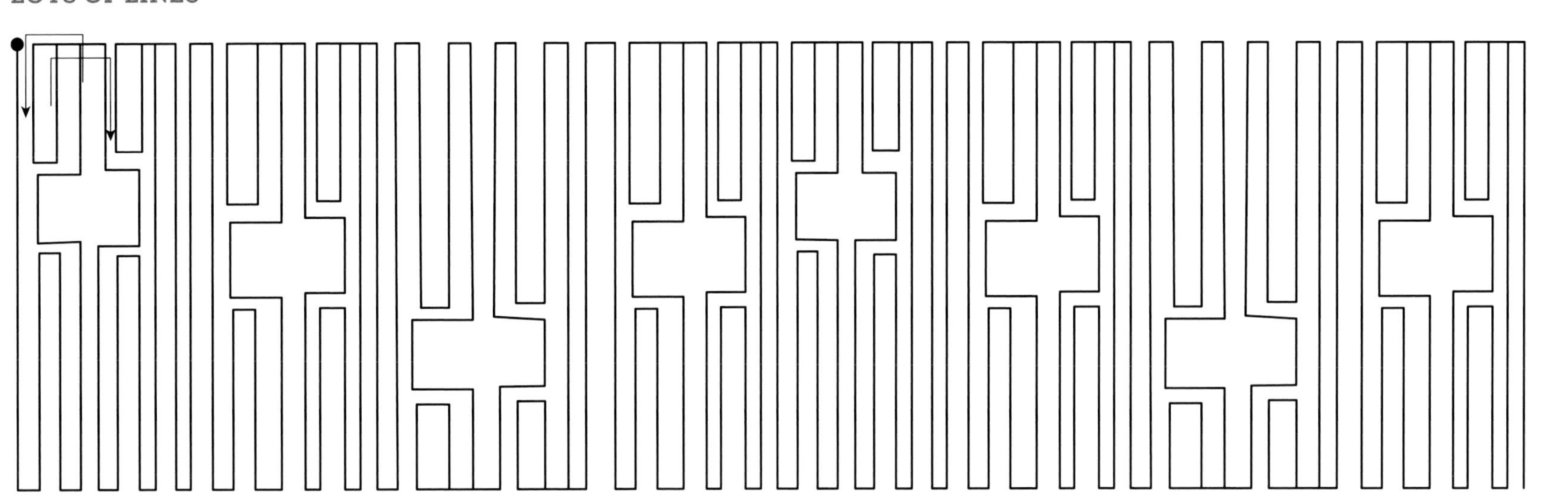

Make parallel lines across the width of the border, occasionally making a wider gap and adding what amounts to Boomerang Squares going one way; then on the next line, finish them, but don't quite close them. There will be backtracking if you want to keep the gaps consistent.

FOREST FLOOR

Use all the Forest Fernies with Curved Spikeys for grass, then travel up the end of the border and make Bark meandering for the sky.

DANDELION FIELD

Use all the Dandelion variations with Curved Spikeys for the grass and a large meander with seed pods attached for the sky. There will be backtracking around the Dandelion Leaves to place the stems where you want them.

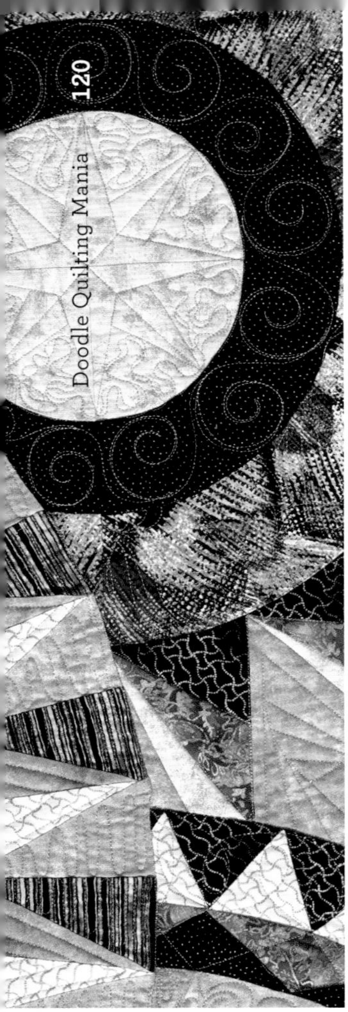

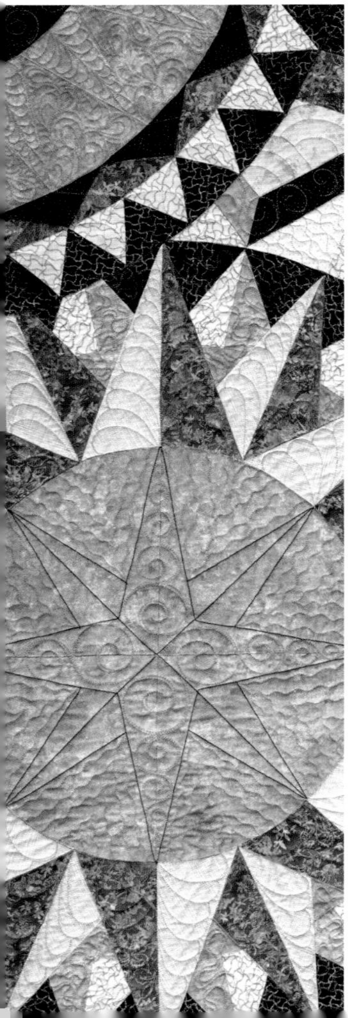

Gallery

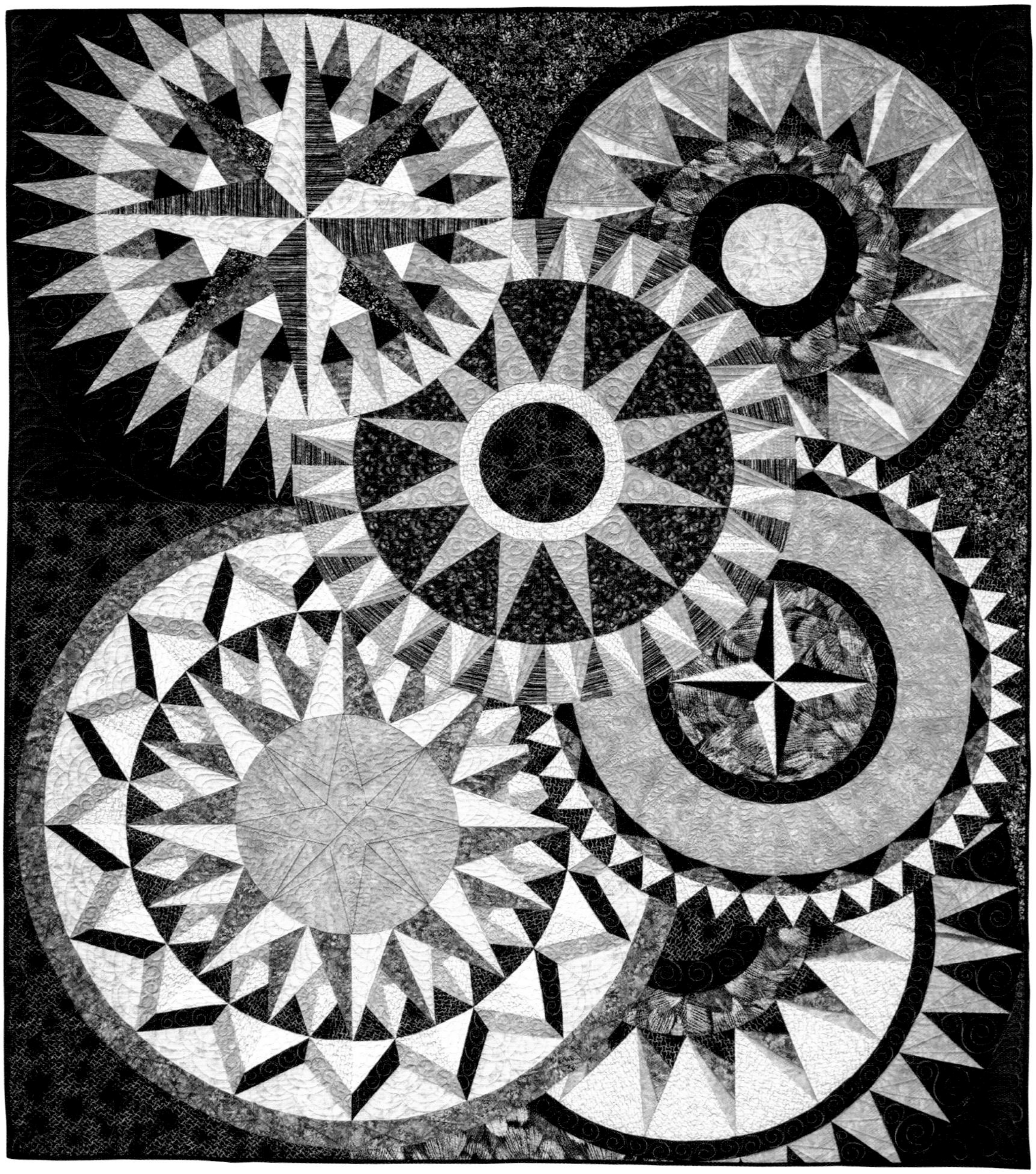

Circular Fascination

My Whirlwind Romance

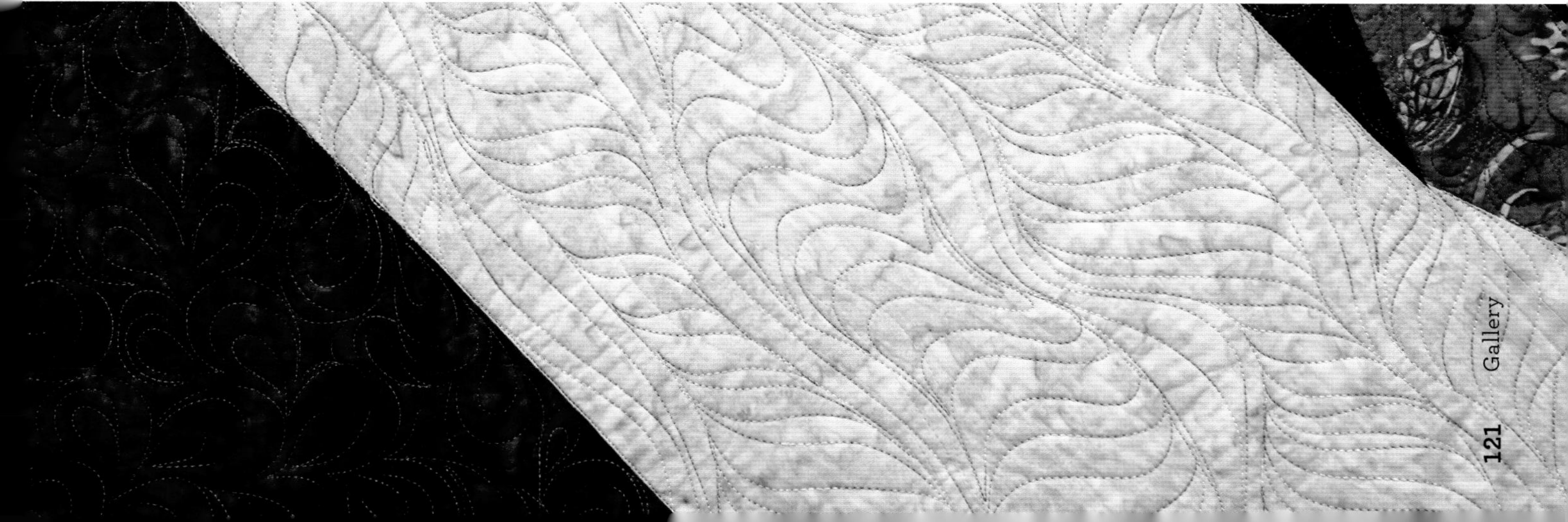

Pieceful Garden

Spring Garden

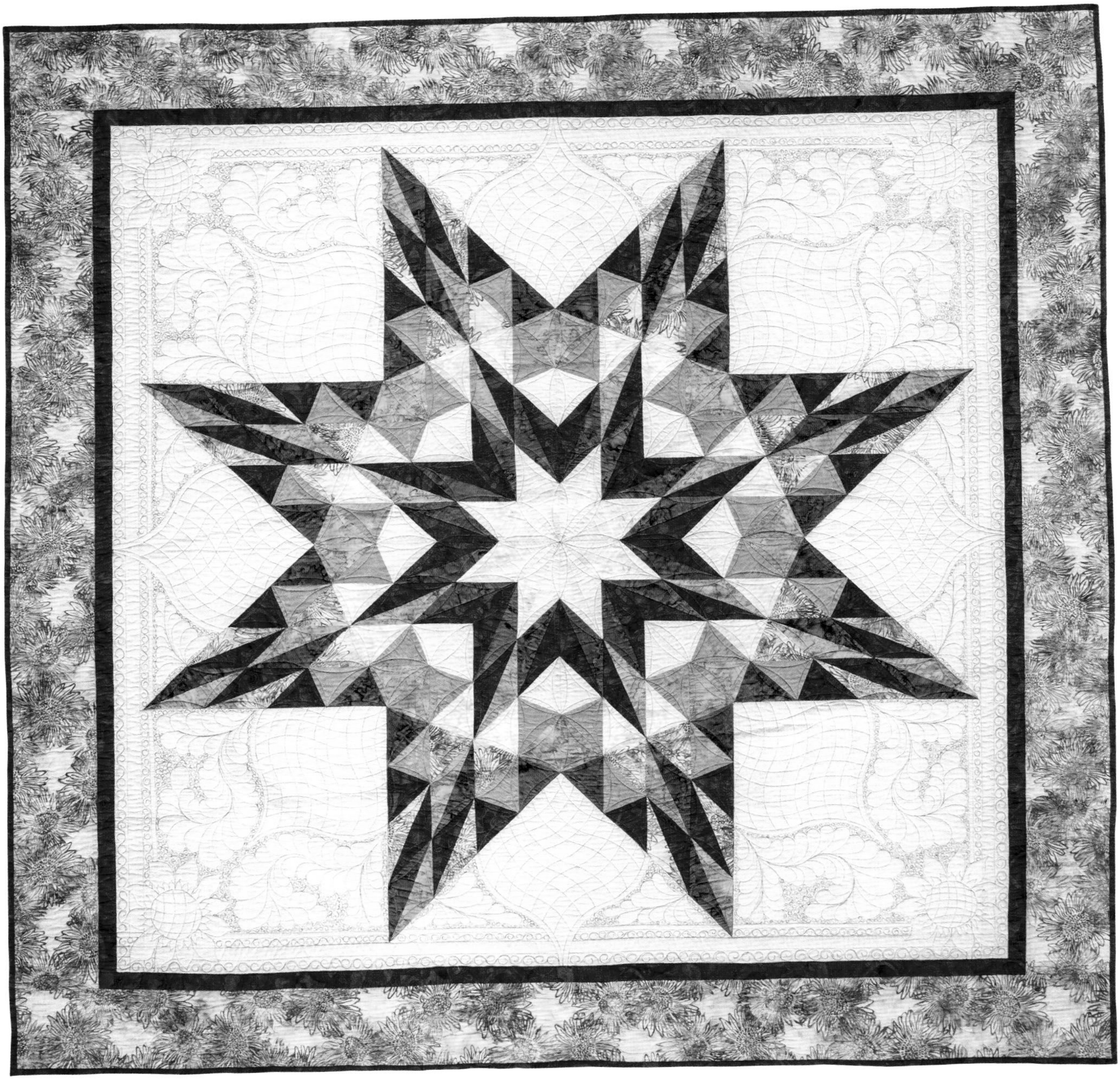

Sunflower Surprise

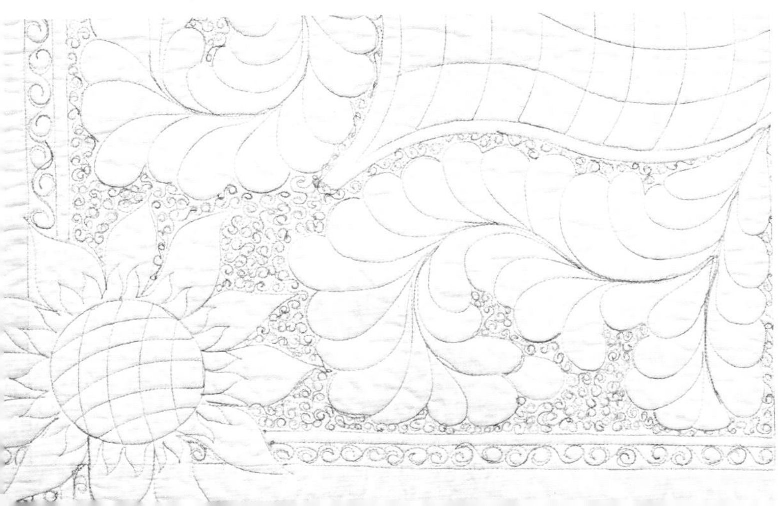

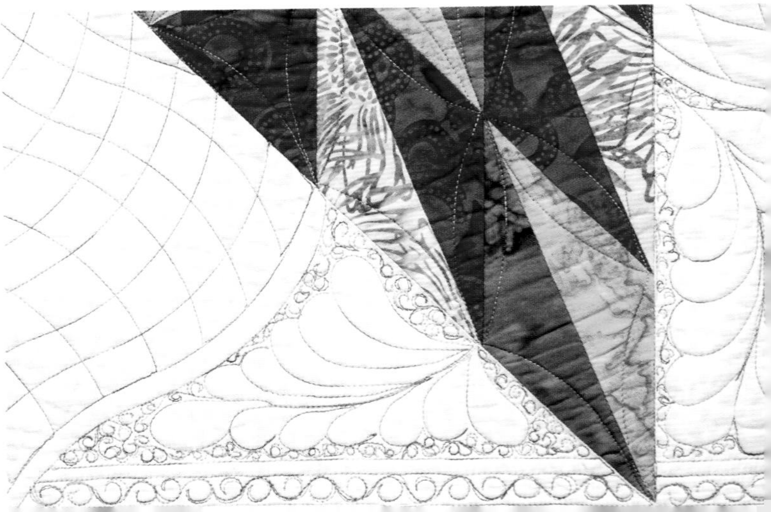

Legend

Here is an overview of the shapes introduced in my book

Doodle Quilting (page 127).

Travelers

Looped Vine

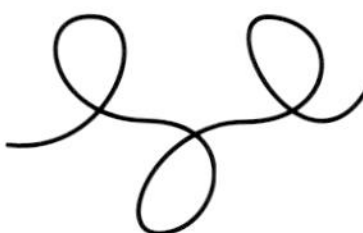

Traveling Circles

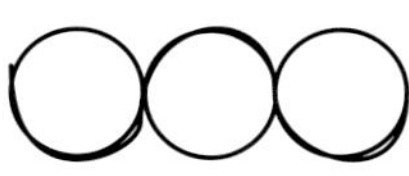

L's

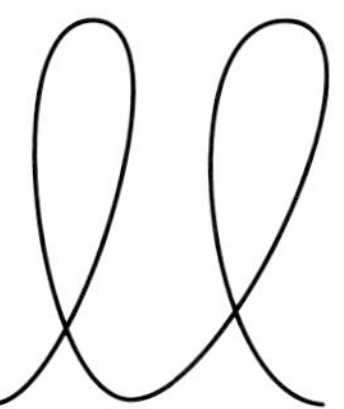

C's or Scrolls

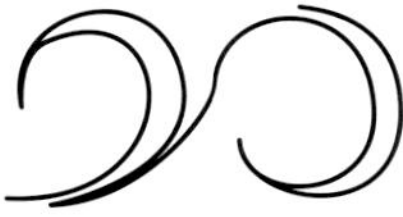

Bark

Teeth

Spikeys

Sunshines

Flower Petals

Excited Water

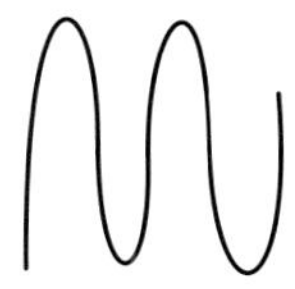

Meander

Double Hook

Round Swirly

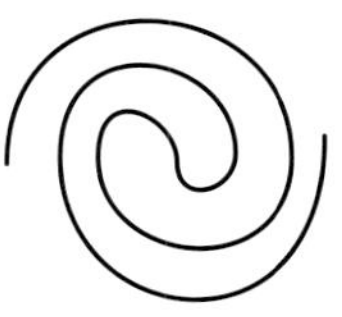

Greek Key

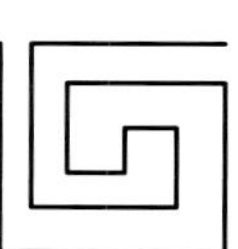

Teardrop 1-2-3

Boomerangs

Simple Leaf

Oak Leaf

Ivy Leaf

Holly

Strawberry

Daisy

Rose

Boomerang Circles

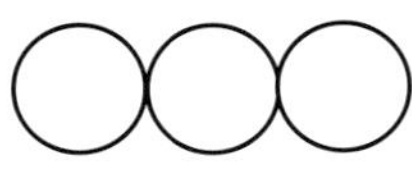

Heart

Teardrop

Ribbon

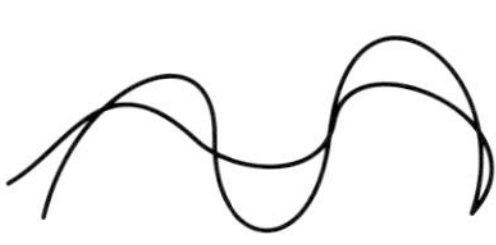

Christmas Tree

Feathers

No-Stem Feathers

Double-Stem Finger Feathers

Victorian Feathers

Eyelet Embellishment

Round Ferny

Forest Ferny

Baby Forest Ferny

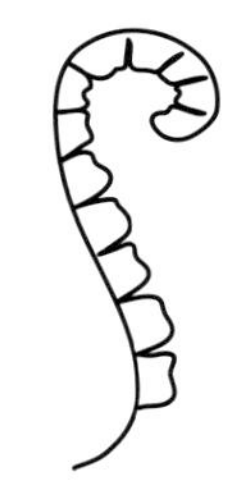

Juvenile Forest Ferny

Palm Ferny

About the Author

Photo by Terry Day

Cheryl Malkowski lives in Roseburg, Oregon, with her husband, Tom, and her dog, Cooper. She loves everything about quilting as long as it can be done with a machine. A quilter since 1993, Cheryl has written six books with C&T Publishing, including *Doodle Quilting*—a best seller—and *Blocks to Diamonds*, which was the beginning of her fascination with complex-looking stars. She has been published several times in magazines, such as *American Patchwork & Quilting*, *Australian Patchwork & Quilting*, and *Fons & Porter's Love of Quilting*, and she has her own pattern company, ***cheryl rose creations***. She works closely with Timeless Treasures Fabrics, designing mostly with their Tonga Batiks. Her first line of fabric came out in 2010 and she's thinking about another. She has been a featured guest on *The Quilt Show* with Alex Anderson and Ricky Tims, as well as *Quilt It! The Longarm Quilting Show*. Cheryl loves to travel and teach.

VISIT CHERYL ONLINE AND FOLLOW ON SOCIAL MEDIA!

Website: cherylmalkowski.com

Facebook: /cherylmalkowski.quilting

Instagram: @cheryl_rose_creations

Pinterest: /cherylmalkowski

Also by Cheryl Malkowski:

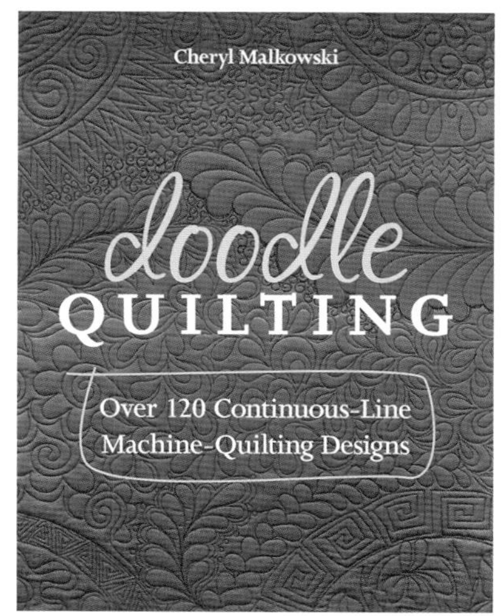

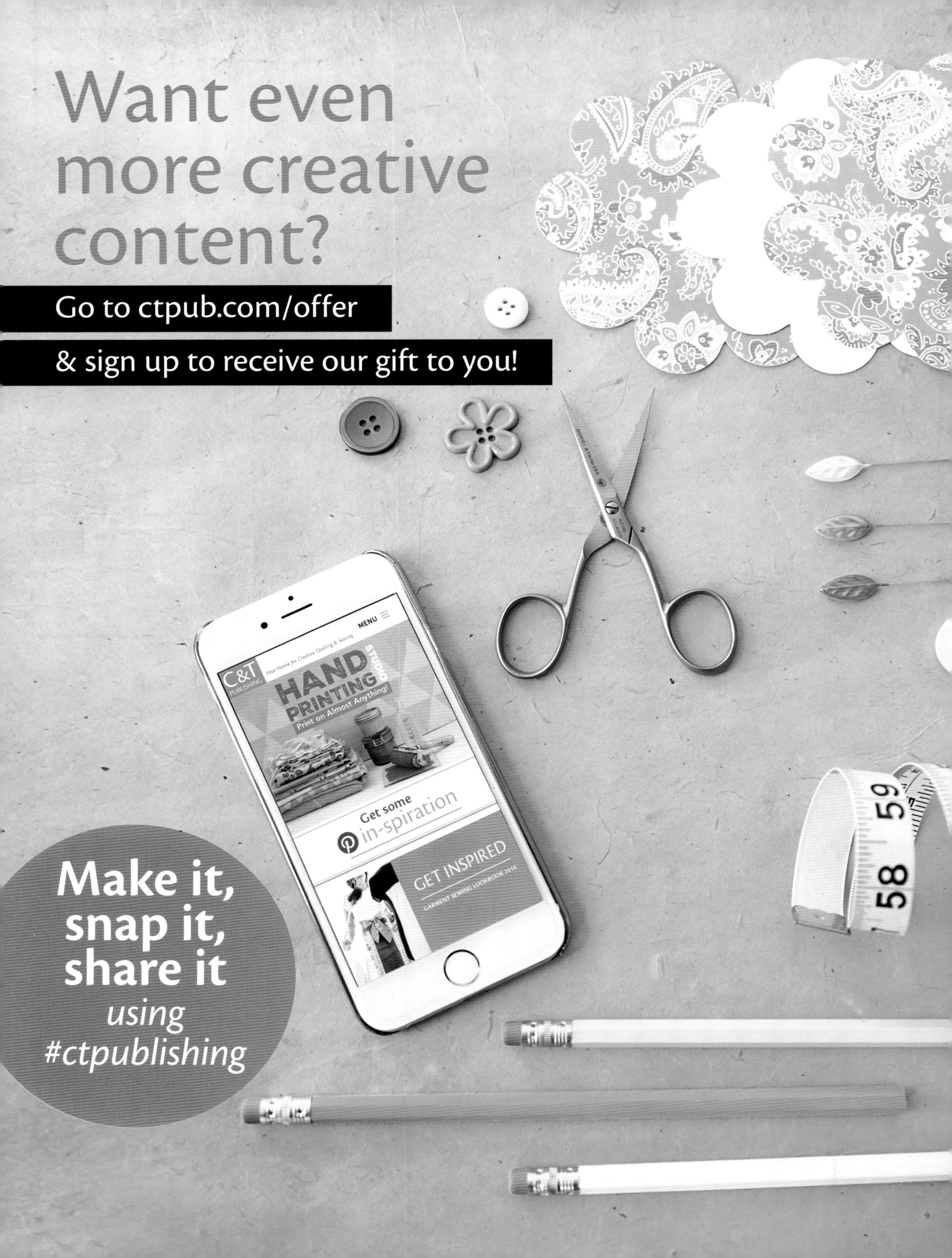

Want even more creative content?
Go to ctpub.com/offer
& sign up to receive our gift to you!
MENU
C&T PUBLISHING
Your Home for Creative Quilting & Sewing
HAND PRINTING STUDIO
Print on Almost Anything!
Get some in-spiration
GET INSPIRED
GARMENT SEWING LOOKBOOK 2016
Make it, snap it, share it
using
#ctpublishing